The Wisdom

to Know

the Difference

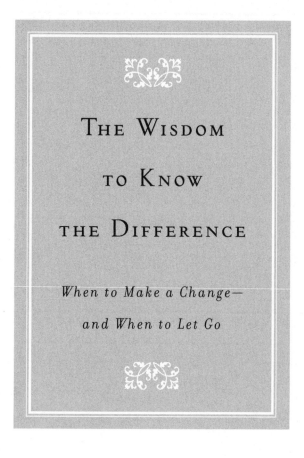

THE WISDOM

TO KNOW

THE DIFFERENCE

When to Make a Change—
and When to Let Go

EILEEN FLANAGAN

JEREMY P. TARCHER/PENGUIN
a member of Penguin Group (USA) Inc.
New York

JEREMY P. TARCHER/PENGUIN
Published by the Penguin Group
Penguin Group (USA) Inc., 375 Hudson Street, New York, New York 10014, USA ·
Penguin Group (Canada), 90 Eglinton Avenue East, Suite 700, Toronto, Ontario M4P 2Y3,
Canada (a division of Pearson Canada Inc.) · Penguin Books Ltd, 80 Strand, London WC2R 0RL,
England · Penguin Ireland, 25 St Stephen's Green, Dublin 2, Ireland (a division of Penguin
Books Ltd) · Penguin Group (Australia), 250 Camberwell Road, Camberwell, Victoria 3124,
Australia (a division of Pearson Australia Group Pty Ltd) · Penguin Books India Pvt Ltd,
11 Community Centre, Panchsheel Park, New Delhi–110 017, India · Penguin Group (NZ),
67 Apollo Drive, Rosedale, North Shore 0632, New Zealand (a division of
Pearson New Zealand Ltd) · Penguin Books (South Africa) (Pty) Ltd,
24 Sturdee Avenue, Rosebank, Johannesburg 2196, South Africa

Penguin Books Ltd, Registered Offices: 80 Strand, London WC2R 0RL, England

Most Tarcher/Penguin books are available at special quantity discounts for bulk purchase
for sales promotions, premiums, fund-raising, and educational needs. Special books or book
excerpts also can be created to fit specific needs. For details, write Penguin Group (USA) Inc.
Special Markets, 375 Hudson Street, New York, NY 10014.

Library of Congress Cataloging-in-Publication Data

Flanagan, Eileen.
The wisdom to know the difference: when to make a change—
and when to let go / Eileen Flanagan.
p.   cm.
Includes bibliographical references.
ISBN 978-1-58542-716-1
1. Change (Psychology)—Religious aspects—Christianity.   2. Providence and
government of God—Christianity.   3. Trust in God.   4. Serenity prayer.   I. Title.
BV4509.5.F53   2009   2009024318
214'.8—dc22

Printed in the United States of America
1   3   5   7   9   10   8   6   4   2

Book design by Meighan Cavanaugh

While the author has made every effort to provide accurate telephone numbers
and Internet addresses at the time of publication, neither the publisher nor the author
assumes any responsibility for errors, or for changes that occur after publication.
Further, the publisher does not have any control over and does not assume any
responsibility for author or third-party websites or their content.

To Megan and Luke,

with love

A NOTE ON THE INTERVIEWS

In some cases the names and identifying details of the interviewees have been changed to protect their privacy or that of other people mentioned in their stories. Although I made a conscious effort to find people of diverse racial and religious backgrounds, I mentioned a person's race or religion only when it was integral to the story being told. When race was relevant, I opted for the labels "black" and "white," although there is still no consensus on which labels come closest to describing the identity of people whose backgrounds are more varied than those labels imply. I use any terms with the understanding that while race is an illusion biologically, it continues to be a reality socially. Many of the people of color whom I interviewed talked about racism as something they needed wisdom to deal with. As a result, the people most likely to be identified by race are people of color, though that does not mean the reader should assume those not so identified are white.

CONTENTS

Introduction   *1*

One

THE COURAGE TO QUESTION   *11*

Two

KNOWING YOURSELF   *47*

Three

SEEKING DIVINE WISDOM   *81*

Four

SHIFTING YOUR PERSPECTIVE   *115*

Five

PRACTICING LOVING ACCEPTANCE   *151*

Six

LETTING GO OF OUTCOMES   *185*

Seven

FINDING WISDOM IN COMMUNITY   *219*

CONCLUSION: WISDOM   *255*

Notes   *261*

Bibliography   *267*

THE WISDOM

TO KNOW

THE DIFFERENCE

INTRODUCTION

I've been told that in olden days, fishermen off the west coast of Ireland never learned to swim, believing that if the God of the Sea wanted to take them there was nothing they could do about it. Even if this is a bit of blarney, it rings true to my impression of my Irish ancestors, who were stoic about death, designing patterned wool sweaters so families could identify lost fishermen when the temperamental Atlantic spit them back unrecognizable. Perhaps it was the shifty weather that made the Irish fatalistic, or the centuries of colonialism, or the particular flavor of religion. My mother often repeated the message given to her in school by a strict nun with a thick brogue: "You were put on this earth to suffer for the glory of Christ, and the sooner you get used to it the better off you'll be." My mother laughed at the nun's message, but I rebelled against it. If I fell off a boat at sea, you can bet I'd swim.

I am American much more than I am Irish, and a daughter of the women's movement rather than colonialism. When I went to Catholic school in the late sixties and early seventies, I had idealistic young nuns who taught me to play the guitar and told me I could be anything. My private high school and prestigious college reinforced this message, so I came to expect success, not suffering. When I experienced my first professional failure at twenty-nine, it was a devastating shock, but one that spurred my spiritual growth. It's been part of my faith journey to learn the spirituality of acceptance, realizing that there are times when letting go and trusting are the best I can do. This does not mean adopting the passivity of the Irish fishermen, surrendering my destiny to fate. It simply means recognizing that while I can chart my own course in life, I don't control the sea around my little boat. I can't guarantee that I won't ever get knocked into the waves, though I can learn to swim in case I do. I've found that recognizing both my power and my powerlessness is useful when facing life's storms.

My recognition of this paradox began when I became pregnant with my first child. I realized I could not prevent my water from breaking in the supermarket or guarantee that my favorite doctor would be on call when I went into labor. More sobering was the realization that I couldn't guarantee my baby's health, no matter how many prenatal vitamins I took. At the same time, my attitude and my choices *did* matter, so I tried to do all the right things. I drank milk instead of coffee and juice instead of wine. I stopped volunteering in a prison because it exposed me to secondhand smoke and took a day-long retreat in the woods to calm my spirit. I knew intuitively that worrying about the baby wouldn't be good for either of us, so I began meditating on the Serenity Prayer, the most famous version of which says:

> *God grant me the serenity to accept the things I cannot change*
> *Courage to change the things I can change,*
> *And wisdom to know the difference.*

The prayer summed up what was for me the major predicament of pregnancy: learning when to passively trust in God (like when I first passed my due date) and when to take action myself (like when my pregnancy went so long as to put the baby at risk and my doctor recommended labor-inducing drugs). The challenge of childbirth—learning when to push and when to just relax and breathe—seemed a fitting metaphor for many other human dilemmas as well.

The same issues were illustrated by my parents' deaths. When my father was dying after years of heart and lung disease, frantic specialists plugged him into more and more machines, even though his mind and heart were shutting down. They did not know when to stop. Their reluctance to accept what they could not change (combined with my father's lack of an advanced directive expressing his wishes) only increased my father's suffering in the end. On the other hand, I also cared for my aging mother, who at one point gave up on life prematurely, suffering unnecessarily for a week before I persuaded her to go to the hospital. I learned that, although we cannot fight death forever, there are times when we're meant to use the power we've been given to save ourselves or someone else. To use the metaphor of the Irish fishermen, there is nothing wrong with swimming when we go overboard or throwing a drowning man a rope, though trying to control the sea is as good a way to drown as doing nothing at all.

The wisdom to know the difference between what we can and cannot change is central to my definition of a well-lived life. When we accept our circumstances, we spare ourselves frustration and anxiety, though we suffer needlessly when we put up with what we shouldn't. Too often, however, we get the equation backward. We feel anxious about not having a perfect figure, while snacking on unhealthy food. We obsessively check the balances of our retirement accounts, while spending money on things we do not need. We try to change other people, instead of changing ourselves. When we get the equation right, putting our energy where it can do the most good, our lives are less stressful and more meaningful. We have more time to make a difference in the world when we're not wasting it on fruitless complaints.

Unfortunately, few voices in our culture help us to develop this wisdom. A glance at the bookstore shelves reveals the problem. On the one hand, most self-help authors preach taking control, arguing that you can become rich or married or thin or smart if you just have the right attitude. One book sums up the self-help creed in capital letters: IF YOU KNOW WHAT YOU WANT, YOU CAN HAVE IT. But what if I want my father to be alive again? What if I want world peace? Knowing what I want will help me to write a book or win an Olympic medal, but it is not always enough. Religious books generally do a much better job of promoting acceptance and serenity, but many go too far the other way, encouraging readers to accept their suffering as unchangeable, even God-given. A few of the Christian books on marriage make sexism sound like a divine gift intended to teach women patience.

The Wisdom to Know the Difference is a different kind of spiritual book, one that argues that it is important to distinguish between letting go and giving up. On the one hand, this book rejects the idea that God decided your lot in life long ago, so if you are poor, or sick, or in a bad marriage, it is because "you were put on this earth to suffer," as my mother's teacher put it. That theology may lead to surrender, but not serenity. It certainly will not empower you to eat well, get marriage counseling, or ask for a raise when one is due. On the other hand, this book also rejects the recently popular pseudospirituality that claims that the universe is a vending machine at your command and you can have whatever you want if you just visualize it, an approach that tends to focus people on their material wants rather than on wisdom.

Instead of accepting these extreme views, I assume that we dance in partnership with a Divine Spirit, which for lack of a better name I call God. Instead of the Lincoln Memorial image of God that I learned as a child, I now conceive God as a loving presence within and around us, available to all, regardless of age or religion. It is my experience that when I move in sync with this Spirit, my life goes more smoothly, for myself and for those around me. Things work out, even when they are difficult. Sometimes I receive a sense of peace or serenity about a situation I am facing. Other times I am given the courage to take action to change what needs changing. In either case, the spiritual guidance I receive produces a better outcome than what I could have figured out on my own. Whatever you call the Divine—and the people interviewed for this book use a variety of names—I'm convinced that listening for its guidance is one key to wisdom.

Throughout this book I make reference to teachings from

Judaism, Christianity, and Islam, as well as Eastern spiritualities, like Buddhism and Taoism. It is not my intention to imply that all spiritual traditions are the same, which would discount the real differences between them, but to simply point out some places where we say similar or complementary things. The struggle to figure out what we should accept and what we should change is universal, and I find it instructive to learn how different people understand it. For example, in Taoism, which began in China two and a half thousand years ago, yin and yang represent two types of energy—one passive, one active—which are interrelated, and need to be in balance. The symbol of two swirls—one white, one black, both containing the seed of the other, flowing endlessly into each other—seems to me a helpful way of representing the relationship between serenity and courage.

While some suspect that the Serenity Prayer has ancient roots, others credit Reinhold Niebuhr, a Protestant theologian known for his concern for social justice. Whether the idea originated with him or not, Niebuhr delivered a sermon during World War II that included a prayer different from the later, more popular version in subtle but important ways:

God, give us grace
To accept with serenity the things that cannot be changed,
Courage to change the things that should be changed,
And wisdom to distinguish the one from the other.

While the "wisdom to know the difference" is catchier, I appreciate Niebuhr's version, which implies that figuring out what we can and cannot change is a process, not a simple formula. It sounds more like discernment.

It is also significant that Niebuhr's version doesn't ask for courage to change what *can* be changed, but for courage to change what *should* be changed. If you think about that for a minute, you'll realize that they are not necessarily the same. There are many things we know should be changed that we simply put up with because change seems so impossible. For Niebuhr, racism, anti-Semitism, and other forms of injustice were clearly on that list. Although Niebuhr was not optimistic about human nature, his prayer asks first for God's grace, inviting us to imagine miracles. Furthermore, it was written in the plural: "God grant *us*." Obviously there are problems that people can tackle together that they could not solve alone. The individual wording more common on coffee mugs and tea towels is pithier than the original, but it relieves the prayer of its bigger challenge, to seek the wisdom to know the difference, not just in personal matters like birth and death, but in social issues, like poverty, injustice, and war.

There are many signs that our world needs wisdom as badly as Niebuhr's did. It seems symbolic that Americans spend more money trying to look young than we spend on educating our young. We also spend more on dieting than on feeding the hungry, although modern agriculture has made feeding the hungry an attainable goal. The irony is that while we chase after ideals that are unattainable, we ignore problems we could solve with a little effort and courage. This isn't entirely accidental. There is a vast advertising industry working around the clock to make us feel we need the latest face cream, or diet pill, or jeans. Keeping us insecure is big business. If we all felt serenity in our lives, we'd be a lot less likely to binge on junk food or mall shopping. Likewise, if we all felt courage, we'd be more likely to ask for a raise or hold our politicians accountable. Instead, many of us in the United States feel politically disempowered, even though legally we have more rights than most people in human history.

Recognizing how our culture has conditioned us is an important part of developing wisdom. Some, like the Irish fishermen, have been taught to accept too much, while others, like my father's doctors, have been taught to strive too hard for control. Becoming aware of the assumptions we've absorbed can help us find a wise balance, though sorting through our cultural conditioning is not always simple. Our gender, race, class, education, personality, and religious upbringing can all affect our sense of power in the world. As a white woman with a working-class upbringing and an Ivy League education, I have experienced feeling powerful and feeling powerless. Like most people, I have faced different challenges in different situations. Still, I've noticed that men and women sometimes need different lessons. It seems no accident that Oprah Winfrey, our era's prophet of empowerment, is a woman, with a mostly female audience.

For those who have been raised to believe that life is in their control, spiritual growth may require learning humility and surrender. Those books about letting go may be really useful. There is an important difference between "letting go and letting God" and playing the victim, however. For those who already feel powerless, religion that glorifies only acceptance and passivity can be abusive, keeping people silent in the face of domestic violence, a groping boss, or unfair pay. Sometimes spiritual growth requires us to work for change, a value supported by feminist and liberation theologies. The people interviewed for this book illustrate this range. Not only do they come from different religions and races, they've experienced different upbringings and challenges. Some needed to learn letting go and acceptance to find wisdom, while others needed to learn courage. The beauty of the Serenity Prayer is that it acknowledges that all people need both, though perhaps in different measures at different times.

When I first imagined this book twelve years ago, I assumed that serenity would be in one section, courage in another, and the conclusion would neatly explain how to discern which was needed when. What I've learned since is that wisdom is seldom so simplistic. Often accepting your circumstances gives you the courage to make needed changes. In fact, both serenity and courage are the fruits of learning to trust and let go of fear. For this reason, *The Wisdom to Know the Difference* is organized around spiritual lessons that can help you live fearlessly: The Courage to Question; Knowing Yourself; Seeking Divine Wisdom; Shifting Your Perspective; Practicing Loving Acceptance; Letting Go of Outcomes; and Finding Wisdom in Community. Each chapter begins with a detailed story that illustrates the chapter's theme, with shorter stories woven in to demonstrate how others have found serenity and courage in the face of a range of challenges, from cancer and divorce to discrimination and global warming.

Throughout this book I also share my own challenges, not because I have always found the perfect balance between action and acceptance, but because I haven't. My learning on this topic has come only partly from books, much more from the messy work of mothering young children, caring for my dying mother, and working for peace. I'm convinced that it's through the struggles and missteps of daily life that we learn wisdom, from practicing serenity when a child needs to go to the emergency room and practicing courage when we see something unfair at work. The purpose of this book is to help you, the reader, reflect on the experiences of your own life so you can tap the source of wisdom within you.

To help you access your own inner wisdom, each section of this book ends with a series of questions. Quakers call these queries and often use them to prompt both individual and group reflection. To examine your responses to the ideas in this book, I recommend that you sit in silence and read each query slowly, leaving time to let answers bubble up from deep within you, rather than rushing to answer the question with your rational mind. If sitting in silence is new and frightening for you, you might start by journaling in response to the queries instead. This can be done individually or with a supportive group. Here are a few questions to help you start thinking about the ideas in this introduction:

What is usually more difficult for you, accepting the things you cannot change or mustering the courage to change the things you should change?

Why is this more difficult?

What would you most like to accept in your own life now?

What would you most like to change in your own life now?

What would you most like to accept or change about the wider world?

What do you hope to get out of this book?

One

THE COURAGE TO QUESTION

Remember why the ancient Irish fishermen never learned to swim? They believed that if the God of the Sea wanted to take them, there was nothing they could do about it. That belief kept them from even trying to save themselves or their companions, at least according to Irish lore. In a sense, their beliefs became as dangerous as the waves.

Your beliefs play a powerful role in shaping your assumptions about what you can and cannot change, and your assumptions, in turn, determine whether or not you even try. Some self-help authors suggest you just change how you think, swatting away disempowering thoughts, but that is harder than it sounds. Your family background, cultural conditioning, and religious beliefs all shape your thoughts, often without your realizing it. This does not mean you are a prisoner of your training, or that one religion is better than another. The purpose is not to cast blame, but simply to understand yourself better so that you can make more conscious choices. Hilary Beard's story illustrates this process.

Hilary was in her late twenties when she realized she wanted to leave her successful corporate career and pursue something creative, like writing. The daughter of a Tuskegee Airman who had worked long hours as Cleveland's top city planner to get his children excellent educations, she had chosen a profession that seemed financially safe, though marketing soft drinks was deadening her spirit. By twenty-eight, she felt she was prostituting herself. Tall and lean with caramel skin and short curly hair, Hilary identifies two keys to finding the courage to change her life: expanding her spiritual beliefs and learning more about her family history.

First, Hilary joined a support group for black women, where she encountered many new ideas. "There were Muslim women, and they thought of God as beneficent," she recalls. "What? God is beneficent?" she responded. "I was raised Catholic and thought God would punish you if you didn't go to confession." Around the same time Hilary went to a Baptist church where everyone was hugged and welcomed, including the prostitutes and drug users from the surrounding neighborhood. "That was the first time I heard, 'Come as you are,'" she recalls. It was also the first time she heard the idea that God could live within her. She gets choked up recalling the effect that message had on her. "God would live in me? I thought God was out there and punishing me," she says with emotion. The possibility of a loving, accessible God started chipping away at her fears of a career change. "I started thinking about who God made me to be and who I was being," she explains. "Why would God have given me these creative gifts if I wasn't supposed to use them?"

As she was reassessing her spiritual beliefs, Hilary began learning more about her family history. Her grandmother had worked her way up from being a domestic and cook to running a successful catering business for some of the richest families of Newport, Rhode Island. As a result, Hilary's father had seen seventy-room mansions and had played with the children who lived in them, though he wasn't allowed to play tennis in their whites-only clubs. He wanted to give his own children the same opportunities as those rich white kids, which was why when Hilary was growing up, he drove her around the mansions near their middle-class Cleveland home and explained to her the kinds of professions that made people wealthy. Creative careers were not on his list, so when Hilary graduated from Princeton, she went the safer route of a corporate career.

On business trips, Hilary started getting to know her father's Southern relatives. She learned that during slavery her great-great-grandmother had cut off her big toe so she wouldn't get sold away from her family, and that her successful Rhode Island grandmother had migrated north alone to get away from the oppression in the South. "I learned all these stories about how courageous they had been," she says, getting choked up when she mentions her mother, who participated in a civil rights sit-in while pregnant with Hilary. "I felt like they were so courageous so I could have any opportunity I wanted, and I was such a coward. It was unacceptable to me, given who I come from. I had to get in my lane. I had to find out what I was supposed to do."

Hilary went to therapy with the goal of mustering the courage to change careers. Early on her therapist—who through serendipity happened to grow up knowing Hilary's grandmother—told her she was a workaholic, like her father, and her grandmother, who had only been a generation out of slavery, a system that forced people to work incessantly. By then Hilary had realized that she wanted to be a writer, but every time she sat down at her computer, she would freeze. "It was too scary to think about becoming a writer because it would be in defiance of my father," she explains. He had given her a strong work ethic and many values she treasured, so it was hard to let go of the values that didn't work for her. "After my dad died, it became difficult to hold the lie together because the person who had created the rules was gone. So the rules started fraying, and I started having trouble at work doing the parts of my job that I didn't enjoy."

Meanwhile in her spiritual support group Hilary was learning new spiritual principles, like the idea that how you think affects what you manifest in your life. She decided to test this concept by imagining the life she really wanted as a writer, making a collage that represented her dreams, and forming a group with a few work colleagues who also wanted to change their lives. "We got together and applied business strategic planning to our personal lives," she explains. "I created objectives, goals, strategies, and measures of success for every area of my life." Going through her objectives, she realized that she had the skills and self-confidence to achieve everything she wanted. The only problem was that she didn't really trust that God would support her if she became an artist.

Then something Hilary's minister said changed her thinking:

"If you're swimming upstream, maybe the problem isn't the stream. Maybe you're heading in the wrong direction." This matched what she was learning in her support group about "going with the flow." "I didn't understand that at all because in my family and in black culture there's all this language around struggle: 'You have to work twice as hard. You have to be twice as good.' I thought struggle was what you were supposed to do." Hilary felt increasingly like she was swimming upstream in her corporate career, so she started "testing things in the direction of the current." She mustered the courage to go to writers' conferences and to take an evening writing course at a local college, where her teacher said, "You may be the best writer I've ever had in one of my classes," comparing her work to *To Kill a Mockingbird*. "With every step I took, the Universe encouraged me," recalls Hilary.

Not every step was easy. Both of Hilary's parents died during the years of her transition, though her father did express support for her new ambition before his passing. After each loss, she took time off from work to grieve and explore what she wanted to do next. Gradually doors started opening. Because of her management experience, she unexpectedly got a job as managing editor of a health magazine for African-Americans. She prayed for an editing mentor, and one appeared. "She was not only the former managing editor of *Essence*, she was the former *New York Times* health editor," explains Hilary, who "saw God's hand in all of these things."

More opportunities came: the chance to edit a diet book that the magazine was publishing, followed by the chance to collaborate on another book. Hilary resigned from her editing job to become a freelance writer; then suddenly her new career stalled.

The book collaboration fell through, and much of her other free-lance work dried up within six months of the terrorist attacks of September 11, 2001, just as the plunge in the stock market lowered Hilary's already decreasing savings. In the face of events beyond her control, she recalls that she really had to make a spiritual choice: "Was I going to believe in fear, or was I going to believe in God?" She decided to trust God, continuing to write, even though for a while it meant depleting her savings.

Hilary's trust was rewarded. In the following years, she found success in part by helping others tell their stories, including tennis champions Venus and Serena Williams and actors Angela Bassett and Courtney B. Vance. Today at forty-five, she has published seven books, two of them bestsellers. She continues to trust that she is on the right path, refusing to let the recent economic downturn make her fearful. She notes that becoming conscious of the ways she was conditioned was crucial to shifting her perspective. "You need to examine what you believe and choose whether you want to believe that, as opposed to it being automatic," she concludes. "God gave us free will, but most of us don't exercise free will because we're on autopilot, following our childhood beliefs. Making a free choice about what to believe is a key to liberating your spirit."

FAMILY INFLUENCES

Hilary learned many valuable lessons from her parents, including a strong work ethic and the ability to dream big, qualities that have continued to serve her as a writer. She also discovered a family legacy of courage that helped her to become courageous herself. More difficult to acknowledge were the family lessons that were not serving her, like the assumption that a creative career could not be financially secure. Most of us have family legacies that are similarly mixed, and reflecting on them will help us to understand our own strengths and weaknesses. Sometimes our parents taught us deliberately, like when Hilary's father drove her around the wealthy neighborhood, encouraging his daughter's ambition. More often, our parents taught us unconsciously through the patterns of their own behavior.

Sophie Williamson grew up with a father who physically abused her older siblings, though he never attacked her. A small woman whose long blond hair and bright blue eyes make her look younger than seventy, she recalls playing the role of witness those many years ago. "I couldn't save my brother and sister, but I would not move," she says firmly. "My mother would leave. I just stood there." Sophie was in her sixties when her father died, prompting flashbacks of his violent attacks and the experience of watching helplessly. By working with a therapist, she processed these memories and came to realize they were the source of the "fix it" impulse that for many years made her waste energy trying to change things she could not change. Becoming aware of where this impulse came from helped her to gradually learn to let go and accept things. Now, when she is next to someone who seems anxious, she just moves away without getting caught up in that person's problems. When she makes a mistake, she simply takes responsibility for it. "Those kinds of things are so much easier," she says. "All of life is easier."

It is not only abuse that we may have to overcome. Sometimes the most well-meaning parents teach us lessons we must later unlearn. The oldest of five children born in quick succession, Marcelle Martin was expected to help her mother and not have many needs herself. She recalls going to school with the mumps because her mother was so busy she didn't realize Marcelle was sick until her younger siblings got the mumps, too. Marcelle laughs about it now, but says the effect was to teach her to be silent. She first noticed this conditioning when she was twelve, during a visit from one of her mother's friends. "One day in the car he was asking me questions, and he really wanted to know what I thought," she recalls. "It was just so moving to me it brought tears to my eyes." It made her realize that her own parents did not encourage her to voice her opinions often. Now in her late forties and a teacher at a spiritual study center, Marcelle notes, "I'm still working on unlearning that one. I'm learning that sometimes I just need to speak my mind."

How your caregivers responded to your childhood requests may have taught you much about what you could or could not change. If your opinion was ignored or never solicited, you may have internalized the sense that what happened to you was beyond your control. You may not speak up for yourself as an adult, even in situations when voicing your concerns might make a difference. On the other hand, if your parents granted your every wish and protected you from every failure, you may have grown up with the unreasonable expectation that you will always get what you want. Learning to accept limits may be your adult challenge.

In his most recent bestseller *Outliers: The Story of Success*, Malcolm Gladwell explores the ways wealthier families train their children to ask for what they want. He tells the story of Robert Oppenheimer, who was nearly kicked out of graduate school for trying to poison his tutor, of all things. Although expulsion would have been a reasonable consequence, Oppenheimer, who came from a family that trained him to assert himself, was able to negotiate a second chance, enabling him to eventually become a famous physicist and the leader of the Manhattan Project, which developed the first atomic bombs. In contrast, Gladwell gives the example of Chris Langan, the smartest man in America, according to IQ tests, but the product of a poor family fraught with domestic violence. When Langan was told that he would lose his college scholarship because his mother forgot to sign a financial aid form, this certified genius simply did not know how to advocate for himself the way Oppenheimer had. Thirty years later, Gladwell describes Langan as still bitter about his brief college experience.

Numerous studies have shown that when people repeatedly experience circumstances that are beyond their control many (but not all) start to assume that everything is beyond their control, so they don't even try to make an impact. For example, Chris Langan, who grew up in an abusive home where he felt powerless, continued to feel powerless when facing the college administrators, even though such a brilliant student could have found other scholarships if he had known how to pursue them. This pattern of behavior, called "learned helplessness," can impact every area of a person's life. I recall a former neighbor who had been beaten down by a challenging childhood, abusive men, and some tragic losses. One day she came home with four rose shrubs and gave me one as a gift. I was touched and carefully followed the instructions that came with it, soaking the roots overnight and planting it in a large hole the next day. My neighbor, meanwhile, left her three shrubs in their bags along our shared walkway without water or soil. After several days and some coaxing from me, she finally stuck them in holes that were too small. When they died soon after, she looked at my thriving rosebush and said ruefully, "I'm not as lucky with plants as you are."

It is hard for people to see when they have created their own bad luck, especially if they have been taught that their actions do not really matter. Psychologists call this having an "external locus of control," the belief that the things that happen to them are determined by luck or God, not their own choices. In contrast, those with an "internal locus of control" believe that their own behavior matters, whether or not they believe in God. It turns out that people's beliefs make a real difference in how they live. For example, those with an internal locus of control are more likely to eat well, exercise, and avoid dangerous behaviors like smoking. Likewise, those who believe their choices make a difference are five times more likely than those who don't to take precautions when they hear a tornado is heading their way. One study showed that tornado deaths in Alabama were significantly higher than in Illinois precisely because Alabamans were more likely to be fatalistic about approaching tornadoes. Research suggests that family and social conditioning influence which kind of locus of control people develop.

Martin Seligman, the bestselling psychologist who first proposed the theory of learned helplessness, went on to become the founder of the movement called Positive Psychology, which focuses on how to build on people's strengths. In *Learned Op-*

timism: How to Change Your Mind and Your Life, he argues that people often interpret problems as being, not only unchangeable, but also exaggeratedly large and their own fault, what he calls the 3 P's, "permanent, pervasive, and personal." So, for example, my neighbor makes a gross generalization, "I'm not lucky with plants," instead of thinking, "I didn't follow the directions that came with those roses." The way she interprets her failure affects not only how she feels but also whether she is likely to do better next time. Seligman says we can retrain our brains to think in ways that are more empowering (a subject that is explored in chapter 4), but first we have to recognize that our reflexive explanations are often distortions: "They are mere bad habits of thought produced by unpleasant experiences in the past—by childhood conflicts, by strict parents, by an overly critical Little League coach, by a big sister's jealousy." How our mothers explained difficulties is particularly influential in determining how we explain them to ourselves later in life.

EXAMINE YOUR EXPLANATORY STYLE

Recall a recent time when something inconvenient happened to you, and try to remember how you explained the problem to yourself. Did you say, "I'm not lucky," or, "Things like this always happen to me"? Did you blame someone else, or did you think of something specific that you could have done differently? ("Oops, I should have refilled the gas tank when I thought of it this morning.") Now think back to how your parents or caregivers explained unfortunate events and see if there are any correlations to how you think today. Did your upbringing foster in you a belief that you can prevent or solve problems, or a tendency to feel that there is nothing you can to do to respond to challenging events but suffer through them?

Having compassion for our parents may be important in coming to peace with our conditioning. Now in his seventies, Melvin Metelits says that when he was young he was "somebody who became very upset, resentful, angry, and fearful at things that had no immediate resolution." In other words, he was not good at accepting the things he could not change and didn't feel much serenity. Sitting in his book-filled apartment, I ask him where his anxiousness came from, and he replies succinctly, "Mom." She was the stereotypical Jewish mother who wanted her son to become a doctor. He explains that her expectations of him were "so straight and so narrow that the least deviation upset her." Melvin notes with sympathy that she was the first daughter of an immigrant family. "She grew up fearful of being persecuted," he explains. "The outside world was anti-Semitic. 'We have to guard against it. Don't deviate. Be Jewish, and be like the others at the same time. Don't do this, you'll get hurt. Don't do that, people won't like you.' That was my mother's craziness, and I had to grow out of that," he recalls.

Instead of a Jewish doctor, Melvin became an atheist and an

elementary schoolteacher. He resented his mother's attempts to control him so much that he didn't see her for twenty years. "Thank God that late in life, I did my repentance with my mother," says Melvin, who also returned to Judaism after taking a class on Jewish identity in his early sixties. He explains that he can now see the beneficial effects of his mother's rigidity. "It made me law-abiding. It made me mindful of other people's feelings. It gave me a sense of boundaries," he says, noting that growing up with no boundaries is just as dangerous as having boundaries that are too rigid. To live with balance and wisdom, he asserts, "We have to unlearn the deep wounds of our parents. We are raised in ways that we have no control over, so we have to cope and along the way pray that there are influences that help us manage the harmful effects of our parents' hurts and wounds."

As Melvin noted, his mother's wounds came, at least partly, from a wider societal problem: anti-Semitism. Realizing this helped Melvin to forgive his mother for the anxiousness she passed on to him. It is important to have this sympathy for our parents, especially if they themselves were affected by societal wrongs. Rachel Yehuda, a professor of psychiatry who specializes in traumatic stress studies, says that trauma can literally be inherited, especially if a woman is pregnant at the time of the ordeal. Speaking of her own research into the biological changes that result from trauma, Yehuda says, "One of the things that hit me straight between the eyes was that the children of Holocaust survivors are particularly vulnerable to mood and anxiety disorders, and to PTSD [post-traumatic stress disorder]." She says that from an evolutionary perspective, parents who have experienced something so terrible are being rational in trying to prepare their children for a dangerous world. "When children realize that their parents were actually trying to give them something to help them cope in a similar adversity, they may understand their childhood differently, and be able to change their own responses to the world to something more appropriate," Yehuda explains.

Recognizing the wider historical context of her father's advice to her helped Hilary Beard appreciate that he was simply trying to help her make it in a sometimes hostile world. His drive to create better opportunities for his children was reflected in other aspects of his life, as well. When he had a stroke during Hilary's senior year of college, he refused to accept the doctors' grim prognosis, continually struggling to surpass their predictions for his recovery, which he did. Although she was inspired by her father's strength, the lesson Hilary needed to learn was to stop struggling so hard and go with the flow more. Having compassion for the circumstances her father faced helped her feel free to make a different choice.

CULTURAL INFLUENCES

Just as recognizing our family conditioning can help us develop wisdom, so, too, can seeing our broader cultural conditioning. Unfortunately, we often don't question cultural assumptions until we are somewhere else, where the assumptions are different. During two and a half years as a Peace Corps volunteer in Botswana, I came to appreciate the "can do" attitude my elite American education had afforded me, as well as the limits of it. There were several occasions when the Peace Corps volunteers at the school where I taught noticed a problem and set about solving it. For instance, because the school's one water spigot was located in a dusty yard with no drainage, it created a giant mud puddle every day when students washed their lunch dishes there. Another Peace Corps volunteer and I applied for a grant to get money for a drainage system, which fixed the problem. Most of my Batswana colleagues didn't have this much individual initiative, but they did have some cultural strengths I lacked, particularly a strong sense of community and an ability to accept the things they couldn't change with a lot more serenity than most Americans.

The more relaxed lifestyle I experienced in Botswana was exemplified by the way people responded to a late train or plane. While Westerners generally started pacing the train platform or airport, Africans tended to take the news of a delayed departure much more in stride, pulling out some food or lying down where they were to rest. In two and a half years some of this calmness must have rubbed off on me. The first time I took an Amtrak train after arriving back in the United States, it was delayed by an hour. My traveling companion, an American professor, remarked that I didn't seem to be bothered by the change in schedule, while he was anxious and frustrated about something he was powerless to change. The ability to go with the flow is one of the things I continue to miss about the people of Botswana, though I suspect their laid-back attitude sometimes kept them from trying to change things like the spigot problem. Like every individual, every culture has its strengths and weaknesses. Americans are known for our ingenuity, but a quarter of our population suffers from anxiety.

Acknowledging cultural differences is tricky business because it is so easy to fall into cultural stereotyping. Obviously, not all Americans are alike, just as not all Batswana are alike, let alone all Africans. Still, our individuality is formed within a cultural context, where some patterns of behavior are more common than others. "Cultural legacies are powerful forces. They have deep roots and long lives," asserts Malcolm Gladwell. "They play such a role in directing attitudes and behavior that we cannot make sense of our world without them."

Although Gladwell's *Outliers* is billed as a book about success, many of its stories deal with the tension between acceptance and initiative that the Serenity Prayer describes, particularly those dealing with cultural legacies. " 'If God does not bring it, the earth will not give it' is a typical Russian proverb," explains Gladwell. "That's the kind of fatalism and pessimism typical of a repressive feudal system, where peasants have no reason to believe in the efficacy of their own work." In contrast, Chinese agriculture is dominated by rice, a crop for which meticulous planning, hard work, and cooperation with other people determine a farmer's output. Hence a typical Chinese proverb advises, "Don't depend on heaven for food, but on your own two hands carrying the load." Such deeply ingrained cultural assumptions impact the way we assess what we can and cannot change, often without us realizing it.

Gladwell does not believe we are prisoners of our cultural conditioning. We can change, he asserts, "But first we have to be frank about a subject that we would all too often rather ignore." *Outliers* recounts a tragic plane crash that happened in part because the Korean copilot came from a culture where it was impolite to correct one's superior, even when the exhausted pilot couldn't see in the dark that he was about to fly into a mountain. Another fatal crash occurred because Colombian pilots, who knew they were running out of fuel on their approach to JFK, did not assert their need to land forcefully enough for the more aggressive New York air traffic controllers to appreciate their plight. "We don't have to throw up our hands in despair," argues Gladwell. Once the airline industry recognized that cultural misunderstanding contributed to these and other crashes, they incorporated this awareness into their training programs. Korean Air, which used to have one of the worst safety records, focused on encouraging frank communication between copilots and pilots and now has one of the best.

Your cultural training is not only a product of your country of birth. Your generation, geographic region, ethnicity, education level, and economic class may also affect how you were conditioned. Tracey Smith-Diggs—who runs pregnancy-prevention programs in difficult urban high schools—can see how societal expectations shape the lives of her students. "They're expected to go out and sell drugs and do this and do that," she observes. "How about those boys who don't want that for themselves? They have to search to find role models." Although Tracey is black like most of her students, she notes that she grew up in a racially diverse, middle-class neighborhood where everyone was expected to go to college. "I don't know what it's like to live in North Philadelphia and pretend you're not smart and not bring your book bag home," she says, referring to the fact that in some neighborhoods students who study hard and want to go to college are ridiculed or bullied for not being cool. "I didn't have to go through that," says Tracey, who had mentors who expected her to work hard and carry herself with respect. She says such high standards shaped who she is today, but notes that her students don't have anyone in their lives with high expectations of them, which makes it difficult for them to expect much from themselves.

In an oft-cited study, education scholar Jean Anyon compared schools that varied by the income and professional level of the students' families. Like the affluent families described by Malcolm Gladwell, the schools of the affluent encouraged students to voice their opinions and think independently, while the schools of the working class encouraged students to follow directions, a skill they would presumably need in the working-class jobs they were expected to perform someday. The differences were apparent in every aspect of education, from the way division and ancient history were taught, to how the teachers managed classroom discipline. I noticed this disparity myself one day when my children and I watched a museum presentation along with students from a low-income neighborhood. I was struck by how focused the teachers were on keeping the first-graders not just quiet but in a straight line, knowing that at my children's private school, the teachers would have put greater emphasis on encouraging the students to ask relevant questions and engage the material.

There are many studies that look at how social conditioning affects the disadvantaged, but fewer that acknowledge the ways it affects the privileged. Consequently, people who are privileged may not see the ways their conditioning sometimes hurts them, too, though being raised to expect complete control can interfere with wisdom as surely as being raised to expect no control at all. Grace Potts, a certified nurse midwife, mentions a stereotype common among nurses, that educated or professional women have a harder time surrendering to the unpredictability of labor than younger, less educated women. "Typically the nursing staff would take an eighteen-year-old over a Ph.D.," notes Grace. "They would say, 'That person's going to be a C-section just because she won't be able to let go.' " Grace thinks this is unfairly prejudicial, though she acknowledges there is truth in it because trying too hard to maintain control can make labor more difficult.

In *A Nation of Wimps: The High Cost of Invasive Parenting*, Hara Estroff Marano argues that many of today's affluent children are so sheltered, they never get to practice dealing with disappointment or failure. "There is abundant evidence that once they leave the protective cocoon of home for college, once they must begin functioning on their own, young people today are breaking down psychologically in record numbers," states Marano. Their parents mean no harm, of course. They just want to keep their children safe and get them into the best colleges possible. Their approach backfires, however, "because it violates the brain's need for meaningful challenge" and denies children the opportunity to learn to handle disappointment. This thesis is supported by other research. One study of a crisis at a U.S. company showed that those who suffered most from the stress of layoffs and job uncertainty—as evidenced by heart attacks, obesity, and divorce—were those who had grown up relatively privileged, while those who had fairly tough childhoods (but not abuse) were generally better at accepting the things they couldn't change and moving on.

Few of us have been trained to have the perfect balance of serenity and courage. The purpose of reflecting on our conditioning is not to blame society, but to understand where we might have room to grow. Knowing what has shaped us is often a first step. However, when I discuss social conditioning with college students I teach, the white middle-class suburban kids often insist that they have no conditioning; they are just "normal." Actually, this is the conditioning that is hardest to see and thus hardest to peel back. People who think their behavior is "just normal" may have an especially hard time acknowledging when their behavior isn't working. No matter what our background, denying that family and cultural patterns have shaped how we deal with issues of acceptance and change is not likely to help us move past our conditioning. Especially if we were encouraged to hide our emotions—training particularly common among boys—we may resist acknowledging the things we would rather not have to change.

Blithely growing up in the wake of the women's movement, I thought I had escaped gender conditioning, until a boss pointed it out to me. In my late twenties, I had worked for a grassroots organization for almost three years and was feeling what activists call "burnout." I wanted time to pursue writing, but felt trapped as the director of a regional office. After I finally got up the nerve to hand in my notice, I got called to meet with our national executive director, a no-nonsense feminist with a black belt in karate, who said something I'll never forget. "You know what makes me frustrated?" she began. "When my male managers are unhappy, they come to me and say, 'I'm unhappy, and here's what I need to make me happy.' But when my female managers are unhappy, they say, 'I quit.' Eileen, what could we have given you that would have made you want to stay?"

"A six-month leave of absence," I said, knowing that no one got that kind of leave.

"Well, that would have been possible," she said to my utter surprise. "Don't you think we'd rather lose you for six months than altogether?"

At that point, I had already made up my mind about leaving, but I remembered her comment and shared it with a friend who was angry when she found out that, as the only female manager in her organization, she was also the lowest paid. When she asked her boss why, he explained, "You were the only one who didn't ask for more than what we offered." My friend and I were both white middle-class women with graduate degrees. We both enjoyed backpacking and world travel. We didn't think of ourselves as helpless types at all. Yet neither of us had considered asking for what we wanted, even though we were valued employees. My boss's observation that this was a pattern among her female managers helped me see how my own social conditioning had included the message that "nice girls" aren't pushy about money, and more subtly, the message that I wasn't worthy of what would have felt to me like special treatment. Much later I learned that learned helplessness is more common among women than men.

Constraining stereotypes may come from not just the people around us but also images in movies and on television. A thirty-four-year-old musician, Will Brock remarks that he doesn't fit either of the most common stereotypes of black men: the thug or the guy in a suit. "I'm not either one," he notes, wearing a red T-shirt, blue jeans, and his hair in thin funky twists. A composer, keyboardist, and vocalist with a busy performing schedule, Will says that stereotypes have still affected his own thoughts. "A couple of years ago I got the bug in my head to be financially responsible and investment savvy," he recalls. The biggest obstacle was his fear that a guy like him—a black kid from the country who did not feel part of the establishment— could not effectively invest, save, and have good credit. Despite this fear, Will started educating himself, reading about investing and finances. This knowledge empowered him, but he says it was a "major head trip" whenever he took a public step, like buying *The Wall Street Journal* at a newsstand or discussing money with people who seemed like they should be more knowledgeable than him. "You feel like you're going to be judged, not on what you understand but on what you look like and how you talk. It was amazing that all of that stuff was in my head. It was just my own trip that I had to push aside because that trip can keep you from growing." Will says that as he learned to invest, his comfort zone expanded, so that he no longer feels uncomfortable with money or the *Wall Street Journal*. Being financially responsible has become the new norm, he explains, but making that change "was a very powerful experience."

Today Will believes that we have a tremendous power to man- ifest positive things in our lives just by changing our thoughts, but he acknowledges that changing our thoughts is not always easy. As it was for Hilary Beard, a key for Will was reexamining his religious training and expanding his ideas about God. "We were taught that God has a plan for you, and that plan can't be altered, like you have no free will. You can't choose anything.

That's not even scriptural," he notes, adding that some people "twist up the Bible verses a little bit" to justify their own power.

RELIGIOUS INFLUENCES

Will is right. Throughout centuries and across faiths there have been those who have misused religion to keep other people down, justifying slavery, sexism, and economic injustice as "God's will." Sometimes people have been told that their problems were the result of their own sinfulness, making it harder for them to muster the courage to change their circumstances. On the other hand, belief in a Power greater than themselves has also brought many people serenity and courage, helping them to cope with adversity, as well as improve their lives. As Roman Catholic priest and scholar Andrew Greeley notes, "Religion has often been a tool in the hands of rulers and a means for cowing people into submission. However, religion has also frequently been a motivating force for those people who feel that they are oppressed." To fully understand your conditioning, it is helpful to reflect on what you were taught about God as a child and evaluate what you believe today.

Like Hilary Beard, Hal Taussig grew up afraid of God, particularly God's ability to judge and inflict punishment. Now eighty-three with a low voice and twinkling eyes, Hal leans back in his chair and recalls growing up an inquisitive child in a family where questioning one's faith was not allowed. "Just believe," his mother would tell him. Then one morning Hal got up early to do chores on his family's cattle ranch. The Rocky Mountain weather seemed strange that morning; the distant steam engine sounded eerie. Looking around and seeing no one else, thirteen-year-old Hal concluded that it was "the Rapture"—the moment, his evangelical family believed, when Christ would transport all true Christians to heaven, leaving everyone else behind to face the terrible "end times." "I didn't go anywhere," he recounts dramatically. Terrified that God had taken his family and left him behind, he ran 150 yards back up to the house before he realized he had just woken up early.

Hal's fear that he would be damned for his questions continued. He began his freshman year at Wheaton College by attending frequent prayer meetings with visiting preachers, though he never answered an altar call, feeling it would be dishonest. "I went through a week of these meetings, and they made me doubt I was a Christian," he recalls. "I remember praying, 'God, I really have been trying to believe, but my doubts often outweigh my belief. I have decided not to try to believe everything in the Bible. I'm quite sure that means I'm going to go to hell.' " Ironically, after praying these words, Hal felt a deep sense of peace. "It was the first prayer that was honest," he explains. After that, he decided he still was a Christian, though not in the narrow definition of his family.

Expanding his idea of faith helped Hal accept a series of professional failures. He had hoped to become a successful cattle rancher like his father, who had built a prize-winning herd by investing in an unusual bull at a bargain price. Instead Hal lost much of his capital on a bull that turned out to be sterile. "It was hard for me to accept the fact that my father was successful and I wasn't," notes Hal, who eventually sold the bull for hamburger meat. "I had kind of an emotional crisis," he recalls. He then went into teaching, which he enjoyed, but that career had setbacks, as well. During one period of unemployment he realized that his worth came from being a child of God, not from his wealth, an insight that helped him to accept his situation and be open to changing careers.

Eventually Hal decided to start a travel business, something he never would have pursued if his cattle business had not failed, but that has brought tremendous financial success. Still believing that his worth comes from being a child of God and not from his wealth, Hal has given millions of dollars to a foundation that is fighting poverty, earning his company Paul Newman's award for the "Most Generous Business in America." Hal explains that he believes he can meet Jesus in any person, so he has to always be on the lookout. "In a way, I didn't give up the return of Jesus. I put a different spin on it," he says with a grin.

Hal's story illustrates some of the fruits of expanding your concept of God. When Hal believed in a distant, judging Lord, he was filled with fear, particularly the fear of going to hell. His faith did not bring him serenity. However, as he began to experience a God who would accept his questions and failures, it made it easier for Hal to accept himself. This self-acceptance, in turn, helped him to accept the things he could not change, like the sterile bull. For several people I interviewed, reexamining their spiritual beliefs led to important, sometimes dramatic, turning points in their lives. Some needed to forget the harsh, judging God of their childhoods, while others needed to admit that there was a Power larger than themselves. For many, acknowledging the Divine within them was crucial. Listening to their stories, I became convinced that expanding your ideas about God can help cultivate both serenity and courage.

Sally Jergesen, for example, was not a religious person, but she started praying when her husband walked out on her and their two-year-old son. A thin thirty-four-year-old with peaches-and-cream skin and a soft voice, Sally explains that after fourteen years of being with him, it has been painful for her to see how quickly her ex-husband jumped into a new relationship. To make matters worse, she feels that during their divorce mediation he intentionally misled her about how much money he would be making in his lucrative new job, prompting Sally to put their son in day care and go back to work full-time sooner than she wished. Although she is still figuring out what she believes about God, she says she has found comfort in self-help books that tell her, "The universe is going to help you and guide you, and you don't need to work so hard. Yeah, you can do things on your own, but you also just have to trust, have some faith that things will work themselves out and that God has something better in mind for you." She explains, "I've been able to hold on to that."

Instead of making her passive, trust in something greater has made Sally more confident in her own abilities. She points out that several years ago when she first took out loans to go to graduate school, several people said not to worry because her husband would be making a lot of money. "Nobody said to me, 'You are an intelligent, resourceful person. You'll be able to take care of yourself.'" The only person who said anything like that was her mother, who had been a single mom herself. Recently a new friend, commiserating about her divorce, said, "You just need to find another rich guy and marry him." Sally responded, "Well,

I have a new strategy in mind—to make a lot of money on my own." Like Hilary, she has found that trusting the universe has been empowering.

Developing trust in something greater may be particularly important for those who were raised to expect too much control. *The Spirituality of Imperfection*, a book that weaves stories from wisdom traditions around the world, argues that "the inherent, eternal, fundamental message of spirituality" is this: *"You cannot control everything. You are a human being, and human beings make mistakes, and that's okay—because you are a human being, not a God."* We live in a culture, the authors point out, that has lost sight of this ancient wisdom, often encouraging people to pursue perfection and control. The result is inevitably frustration and angst. "Anxious determination to take control, to be in charge, reveals the failure of spirituality," they argue. Instead of *willfulness*, the authors explain, we need *willingness*, an openness to letting life surprise and change us.

The success of Alcoholics Anonymous demonstrates how *willingness* to change can be more effective than *willfulness*. One of the founders of the organization that made the Serenity Prayer so famous, Bill W, recalls the realization that he could not control his alcoholism through willpower: "It was a devastating blow to my pride." As a young man, Bill had been unusually confident and ambitious, but after ruining his business, his health, and his marriage, he gave up all hope of controlling his drinking. "I who had thought so well of myself and my abilities, of my capacity to surmount obstacles, was cornered at last," he writes. "Alcohol was my master." Ironically, admitting he was powerless over alcohol was the first step in his recovery because it enabled him to open himself to a "Creative Intelligence" more powerful than himself, despite being critical of traditional religion. With the support of a fellow alcoholic, Bill accepted what he couldn't change—the effects of alcohol on his mind and body—and ceased drinking forever. Convinced that only a spiritual approach to alcoholism could be successful, Bill and his new friend began sharing their experiences with other alcoholics, thus helping to launch a worldwide recovery movement.

Because AA does not try to define God—using instead the term "Higher Power"—it has been able to reach people from a wide variety of backgrounds, including those who feel alienated from traditional religion. That was the case for Matthew Cole when a counselor first suggested he might have a drinking problem. "For a long time, I couldn't relate to God," Matthew recalls, sitting at the kitchen table where he often says his morning prayers. "Then after twenty years of alcoholic drinking, I went to Alcoholics Anonymous. Early on I heard people referring to God as 'Good Orderly Direction.' " That childlike description made more sense to him than the abstract concepts he had heard in church growing up. "Somewhere around me, all of the time, there is some sort of Good Orderly Direction, even in chaos, that I can find within me or hear from others," he explains. That realization, along with a community of supportive people, saved his life. As soon as he went to AA at the age of thirty-two, he stopped drinking, and hasn't drunk or smoked pot in the seventeen years since. Now a sponsor, someone who helps others to stay sober, Matthew explains that he'll often recite the Serenity Prayer several times a day, though sometimes he only needs to say it once for it to bring him peace. A computer technician by training, he notes that there could be some scientific explanation for the calming effect that repeating a prayer has; all he knows for sure is that it works.

For some, it is not a matter of accepting a Higher Power, but expanding the picture of God they developed during childhood. David Watt, an associate professor of history and adjunct professor of religion with short white hair and a cropped beard, grew up the son of a Southern Baptist minister. "A turning point in my life was going to an Episcopal church, and there was this very beautiful, smart woman priest who for some reason was delivering her homily while sitting down," recalls David, noting that in the Episcopal Church the priest is really representing God. "Halfway through the homily, her daughter came and sat on her lap, which was the most powerful rejiggering of God for me." David had always thought of God as a father figure, and while that metaphor is still meaningful to him, he now says "the more metaphors the better" because no one image can fully capture God. "Now what I am struggling with is an understanding of God that completely abandons the idea that some things are sacred and some things aren't. I'm trying to understand what it would be like to really live as if I were as close to God as the branch of a vine." He notes that during those moments when he does feel so connected, he does not get anxious, which he is prone to do when he is feeling disconnected.

Roman Catholic priest and scholar Andrew Greeley asserts that how we conceive of and describe God has profound implications for how we live. A sociologist interested in the intersection of religion and culture, Greeley has developed a tool he calls the Grace Scale "that measures a respondent's image of

God as mother versus father, lover versus judge, spouse versus master, and friend versus king." Greeley's research shows that a high score on the Grace Scale predicts many other qualities, as well, including interest in the fine arts, belief in the equality of women, satisfaction in marriage, compassion for people with AIDS, and willingness to invest in protecting the environment. In other words, how we see God has profound implications for how we see ourselves, other people, and our world.

Many religions recognize that one image of the Divine does not suffice. Muslims have ninety-nine names for God, a deity that is beneficent and merciful, as well as powerful and wise. Likewise, the ancient Hebrews recorded sixty different names for the Divine as a way to get around the one name they were forbidden to say. These names have different connotations: some male, some female, some implying a distant or transcendent God "out there," and others implying a closer, more immanent God that can be found "right here." The idea that God is near as well as far goes back thousands of years, running through Hinduism, Judaism, Christianity, and many indigenous religions. Although there have sometimes been tensions between those who believe in an immanent God and those who believe God is only transcendent, the truth is that different people may experience different aspects of the Divine at different points in their lives. Spiritual teacher William Kreidler once said that he never pictured God as a father figure until he got AIDS. "Then I needed a God with arms," he confided, "because I needed to be held."

"People experience God in profoundly different ways," notes thirty-five-year-old rabbi Erin Hirsh. "If we can celebrate how many ways people can experience God, then we can be united in that, and God doesn't have to be divisive." Rabbi Erin, who grew up in a secular Jewish family, says she experiences God in moments of profound connection with other people. "It took me a long time to understand that, but I believe that there are sparks of the Divine in each person. When I connect with someone, and I find that spark, I've seen a glimpse of the Divine." She says that she is unusual for a rabbi in that she does not think of God as a supernatural being, but she notes that in Judaism, people are expected to wrestle with tradition, with scripture, and even with God, the way Jacob wrestled with a mysterious angel before he was granted the name Israel, or "God-wrestler." When she is teaching children, Erin invites them to join this tradition of wrestling, taking a biblical text and seeing how they can connect to it, whether it is seeing a story literally or allegorically.

Wrestling with your tradition, including its scriptural texts, is a way of being in profound relationship with it. Rather than being disrespectful, it means taking it seriously, acknowledging its strength. Unlike the children in Rabbi Erin's congregation, however, many children are taught to accept scripture as literal truth, with no room for questions. Especially when this is combined with an acute fear of judgment, it can be frightening for such children to question what they have been taught. Even in adulthood, the fear can linger much longer than the beliefs, keeping people from finding the serenity and courage that trust in a Higher Power can bring.

Will Brock says he always wrestled with the literal interpretation of the Bible espoused in his family's Baptist church.

He recalls being ten or eleven and trying to reconcile the creation story with the dinosaurs he was learning about in school. It seemed to him that most people just believed what the pastor told them, while he was always questioning and testing what he heard against his own experience. Will still uses the term "God" and the pronoun "He," but he no longer thinks of God as a person, and certainly not one whose focus is on judging. "It's not some Dude sitting on high, looking down at the world," as he imagined as a child. "It's just the well from which we all came," he asserts. Moving past the old caricature is not always easy, however. "We're so conditioned," notes Will. "I say these things and get chills because it scares me. It might be the Dude sitting there looking down." He makes a stern father face. "I still have that in the back of my head because of my entire life's training, like I might need to go to the gate and explain this conversation."

Despite having left his family's faith, prayer and scripture are still meaningful to Will, including phrases like "He walks with you wherever you go." "You're part of God, so of course God walks with you," he says. For Will, expanding his idea of God has helped him to acknowledge his own power to change his circumstances, building a successful career as a musician, although everyone in his small town thought that was a crazy dream.

One theme that runs through these stories is the idea of an indwelling God, a Spirit that not only can be accessed by people, but makes people themselves holy, as David Watt put it, "like the branch of a vine." It takes the concept of an immanent, present God one step further, though people may have different theological understandings of the root of our sacredness. Buddhists talk of our "Buddha nature," while Muslims speak of *fitrah*, the essential goodness we are born with. Rabbi Erin called it "sparks of the Divine." Hilary Beard heard it as "God living in me," while Will described it as being "part of God." Quakers use a variety of terms to describe this aspect of the Divine: the Inner Light, the Inward Teacher, or the Inner Christ, to name a few. In fact, the belief that there is something of God in every person is one of the hallmarks of Quakerism and the source of the Quaker beliefs in nonviolence and equality, though promoting this idea got the early Quakers imprisoned and tortured in seventeenth-century England. The rulers of that hierarchical society recognized that people who believed they had direct access to God might feel empowered to challenge their authority.

It is an empowering idea, and part of what attracted me to Quakerism as an adult. I had left the Catholic Church during my freshman year of college after realizing that I wasn't sure I believed everything in the Profession of Faith and didn't want to recite something I didn't believe. For several years I felt a sense of connection to something larger in the forest or the mountains, but wasn't sure what to call this experience. Then in my late twenties—when I was struggling to acknowledge my unhappiness in the activist job I mentioned earlier—I felt drawn to start attending a Quaker meeting (the word we use for congregation). Because I had gone to a Quaker (or Friends) high school, I was familiar with unprogrammed worship, with no priest or creed. I could sit in silence with my questions without having to profess any answers. I soon found that sitting in silence forced me to face my dissatisfaction at work, while opening myself to the possibility of a Higher Power bolstered my courage to change careers and start writing.

Finding my own path was profoundly important, bringing me a much deeper faith than I would have felt if I had never allowed myself to doubt what I had been taught as a child. For my mother, however, watching me reject her tradition was painful. First, she prayed that I would return to the church. When that seemed unlikely, she and my aunt prayed that I would at least marry a Catholic so any children I might have would be baptized. Her second prayer was answered when I married a wonderful Catholic man whose deep commitment to his faith has helped me see many of the positive aspects of the church I left. I rejoice that my children are being raised both Catholic and Quaker, though that only partly made up for my lapse in my mother's eyes. For my family, IrishCatholic was one word, the label that defined us, that separated us from the British, who colonized our homeland. By leaving the Roman Catholic Church and joining a religion that began in England, I committed a tribal betrayal.

Knowing how difficult it was for me to find my own belief system apart from my family's, I was intrigued to find that many of the people I interviewed had gone through something similar, whether they ultimately changed religions or stayed within the tradition in which they had been raised. I had set out looking for people who seemed wise, or who had an interesting story to share. It turned out that a turning point in those stories was often looking within themselves to find their own answers. It was part of a journey of finding themselves, the subject of the next chapter.

When you were a child, did the adults around you encourage you to voice your preferences, or not?

What did you learn about your ability to influence the world around you?

What aspect of your cultural conditioning has affected you the most?

Has this conditioning made it easier for you to accept the things you cannot change, or change the things you should change?

Did you believe in God as a child? If so, what did you think God was like?

Have you questioned your childhood assumptions? If not, why not?

What do you believe now about the Divine (or whatever word is most comfortable for you)?

How do your beliefs affect how you live?

Two

KNOWING YOURSELF

As Marcelle Martin shared in chapter 1, saying what she thought and felt was not usually encouraged in the busy family of her childhood, so learning to excavate her own truth has been an ongoing process. Today she teaches classes like "Discerning Our Calls" at Pendle Hill, a spiritual study center in southeastern Pennsylvania, where she lives and works. She writes mostly about prayer and the mystical experiences of women with prophetic callings. Coming to know herself has strengthened her work and helped her learn when she should make a change and when she should let go.

From age five, Marcelle knew she wanted to be a writer, though people had warned her that she wouldn't be able to support herself this way, so in junior high she came up with the idea of working as a psychiatrist part-time to support her writing. Laughing now because she didn't understand how much training a psychiatrist needs, she explains, "That was the only image I had of someone who meets with people to explore their inner lives." By the time she graduated from Swarthmore College, Marcelle had a clearer sense that her calling was to nurture people's spirits, whether through writing or teaching, and that taking a conventional job might sweep her into a career that wasn't really her calling. "I made a vow that I would never take a full-time job unless it was my vocation," she says, "though I might have to take a part-time job to support myself."

Marcelle made other unconventional choices, as well. She recalls receiving a marriage proposal after college from a lonely man she didn't know that well. "He said, 'You want to be a writer, and supporting you while you write will give my life meaning.'" Marcelle laughs again. "Since my boyfriend had broken up with me, and I was sad and depressed, there was a tiny bit of temptation," she says with a smile. Although she finds it funny now, the incident made her realize how easy it would be to marry for the wrong reasons. "I made another vow that I would never marry anyone unless I had a very certain feeling in the pit of my stomach that it was the right thing. So I haven't been married yet," she notes.

Although she has not married, romantic relationships have been an important part of Marcelle's spiritual journey, helping her to get in touch with her emotions and intuition. She recalls in graduate school feeling a fierce attraction to a man she knew rationally was a poor choice and having to pay attention to the fact that her thoughts and feelings were out of sync. "The relationship didn't last very long, and it was really kind of miserable, but it got me in touch with other parts of myself and led to a spiritual awakening," she notes. "That experience opened up so many questions that I had to start seeking spiritual answers. It was a very big turning point."

For eight years Marcelle studied an intensive meditation practice that involved focusing on an emotion, going deeper to discover what was behind it, and then releasing the energy. "If you stayed with the layers of emotion and let the energy be as intense as it wanted to be, it would eventually take you back to some understanding or insight," she explains. Although she no longer practices this type of meditation, Marcelle still finds it helpful to pay attention to her emotions and explore what is beneath them. "By peeling back through all the layers, I get back in closer touch with my connection with God, which comes from a place of love, peace, wholeness, and understanding." When something happens that makes her feel afraid or separate, she has to go through the process of facing it, which is not always quick or easy, because burying her emotions only alienates her from God.

Marcelle gives the example of another romantic relationship in which she buried some of her feelings in order to avoid conflict with a partner whom she hoped to marry. "I reverted to my childhood pattern of when there was friction, mostly suppressing parts of myself," which she notes was the less courageous option. "It was also the option that allowed me to keep the romance for as long as I did, but eventually I realized that was killing me—I mean literally." Marcelle often gets signals from her body when she is suppressing some truth. This time, she started feeling a pain in her heart and having disturbing dreams. She started taking more time to meditate and pray by herself in the mornings to find out what was going on. "One morning at the end of the hour,

I heard a message, 'You might cheat your heart, but your heart won't cheat you.' The pain in my heart was saying, 'Something is not right here. You're cheating yourself.' "

That message prompted Marcelle to begin looking at how she was denying parts of herself to keep her romantic relationship harmonious. "Taking retreats was very important," she recalls. "It was amazing how by physically removing myself from that situation and that relationship, I was able to see things that I couldn't when I was there. Each time I went away, I came back with a little piece of clarity." She gradually started being more authentic, saying what she thought and felt, even when it risked alienating or angering her partner. "That caused a lot more friction," she recalls. "Eventually I realized I needed to leave that situation. So that was a hard lesson, but good." Overall, she says, the relationship brought her much positive growth, even though it did not end in marriage, as she had originally hoped.

The two vows Marcelle made when she was in her twenties have freed her to follow her deepest desires, instead of just social expectations. Although she often had to live simply and share housing with friends to make ends meet, working only part-time gave her time to devote to her spiritual development and writing. Teaching at Pendle Hill—which she describes as her dream job—is the first full-time position she has had. "I can't think of any other way I could have gotten here other than the way I did," she notes. "That meant that for many years it looked like I was doing something really weird." She recalls people telling her, "You're getting middle-aged. You really should have a job with health insurance." Sometimes there were employment opportunities, and she was tempted. "But I thought, 'If I take a job that

I don't want in order to get health insurance, then I'm going to need the health insurance because I'm going to get sick!' " By listening to her body and her feelings, she has been able to make choices that are in harmony with her True Self, if not always with her culture.

Marcelle points out that many spiritual writers describe the True Self as the person you were created to be, before all the experiences that taught you to hide your self. She says that in many ways the spiritual journey "is about coming to know your self more truly, knowing yourself in connection with God, realizing that deeply, truly what you want is the same thing as what God wants, and being open to letting God make that happen."

SELF-KNOWLEDGE, A KEY TO SERENITY

Marcelle's story illustrates how self-knowledge relates to the wisdom to know the difference. Like Marcelle, you cannot change how you were raised or what messages you received as a child. You can, however, become conscious of what those messages were and work to overcome them. You cannot control your emotions or banish painful feelings from your life, but you can face your painful feelings when you have them so they do not control you unconsciously. If you avoid facing them, if you choose to simply suppress your difficult emotions, you will never find serenity because those emotions will continue to eat away at you from the inside, manifesting in anxiety, depression, or even physical symptoms. You will also block out the wisdom telling you to leave an unhealthy relationship or turn down a job that is not your calling if you deny how you really feel. Getting in touch with what is going on inside you is crucial to sorting out what you should accept and what you should change.

Instead of listening to who we really are, many of us model our lives on social norms, getting married or taking a conventional job simply because that is what is expected. We may even assume it is what God expects of us. Yet many religious teachers have said that knowing who you are, rather than trying to be someone else, is essential to fulfilling your purpose. A Sufi story illustrates why we can't just imitate someone else's journey; we need to know who we are in order to know how assertive or passive to be:

A man walking through the forest saw a fox that had lost its legs, and he wondered how it lived. Then he saw a tiger come up with game in its mouth. The tiger ate its fill and left the rest of the meat for the fox.

The next day God fed the fox by means of the same tiger. The man began to wonder at God's greatness and said to himself, "I too shall just rest in a corner with full trust in the Lord and he will provide me with all I need."

He did this for many days but nothing happened, and he was almost at death's door when he heard a voice say, "O you who are in the path of error, open your eyes to the truth! Stop imitating the disabled fox and follow the example of the tiger."

In a similar vein, a Jewish story tells of a man who tried his whole life to imitate Moses, but when he died God told him, "I didn't need another Moses. I needed you." The message is clear:

you cannot change who God made you to be, but if you accept it, you can change the ways in which you are not living as your True Self.

The ancient Chinese philosophy of Taoism teaches the principle of Inner Nature. Each thing, or person, has its own unique attributes. You can try changing a thing's Inner Nature, but it will be a waste of energy. Instead it is wiser to change your expectation of it. As one Taoist story puts it, a man was complaining about a large tree he owned that was too crooked to be used as lumber. He said the tree was useless. A wise man responded that the problem was not the tree. The problem was that the man was trying to use it in the wrong way. Instead of being meant for lumber, it was meant for shade. This story illustrates the wisdom to know the difference at its simplest. Instead of trying to straighten a crooked tree, use it for shade. Unfortunately many people spend a lot of time trying to force things to be what they are not, including themselves. As Benjamin Hoff explains in *The Tao of Pooh*:

> Everything has its own Inner Nature. Unlike other forms of life, though, people are easily led away from what's right for them, because people have Brain, and Brain can be fooled. Inner Nature, when relied on, cannot be fooled. But many people do not look at it or listen to it, and consequently do not understand themselves very much. Having little understanding of themselves, they have little respect for themselves, and are therefore easily influenced by others.

It is easy to be influenced by others. Human beings are social animals. We want to fit in. We want to please the people around us, or at least not be rejected by them. Unfortunately the fear of being rejected can prompt us to suppress our Inner Nature, which some authors have called our True Self. Instead of being a shade tree, we try to twist ourselves into lumber, if that is what our family or culture values more. We present a False Self to the world in order to get the world's approval, but at great personal expense, for once we suppress one part of ourselves, other parts are inevitably hidden, as well.

Timothy Olsen recalls how hiding his attraction to other men kept him from fully relating to God or other people. "My teenage years were literal hell," he recalls. "I was battling fear." A devout Episcopalian, he complained to God, "Why did you make me this way? I just want to be normal." Through this turmoil there were a few scripture stories that helped. First, there was the model of Jacob wrestling an angel of God. "In the end there's a blessing," Timothy notes. "There's also a dislocated hip, but there's a blessing and a new name. For me, the new name was 'You are gay. You're a child of mine, and you're gay.' " Timothy also found reassurance in the story of Amos telling people he was "a dresser of sycamore trees," rather than a prophet or a prophet's son. The message he took from it was, "I'm not what you want me to be, but I am who I am, and I'll do the best I can." He finally "settled down and said, 'Okay, God made me this way and I can't change what God made.' "

Accepting the truth of his sexual orientation helped Timothy to live with less fear in all areas of his life, particularly his relationships with other people. "All my life I felt that my family would reject me and hate me because of this," he recalls. "The reality has been that they love me, support me, and care for me as much [as] and in some ways more than they did before I came out to them." He realizes now that he suffered needlessly because of his own fear. "The cloud was hanging over me," he notes. "It wasn't hanging over the rest of the family. It was hanging over me. When I let the cloud blow away—it's corny, but the sunlight shone upon me." Being honest about who he was enabled Timothy to have a much closer relationship with his father, in particular, and helped him feel a deeper spiritual connection with God.

Unfortunately, fear keeps many people from being honest with themselves or others. I remember one young man I knew in college telling me that his father wanted him to go to law school, and his mother wanted him to go to business school. "I think I'll go to business school because I like my mom better," he said. I asked what he wanted to do, but he brushed off the question. After some prompting, he confided almost in a whisper that he secretly wanted to be a third-grade teacher. When I said he would be a wonderful teacher, I could see the mask of the False Self jerked back into place. No, he said, his family would never accept that. This young man came from a wealthy family and had a large trust fund waiting for him, so it was not that he needed a high-paying job to pay off his college loans. He already had the "financial freedom" most people dream of, as well as excellent grades from a top university. The problem was that being a teacher wasn't high enough status for the son of a successful attorney. Later I heard that the young man had gone to law school, like his father.

The young man might have accepted this career, but often when we accept something we shouldn't, we feel resignation, rather than serenity. We become resentful or restless, though we may not admit it, even to ourselves. If we don't muster the courage to look at our lives and make a change, we may eventually get ulcers or high blood pressure. The problem isn't the law, or whatever other profession we've gotten sucked into. Being a lawyer is only wrong if it doesn't allow us to be true to ourselves. For some the law might be the perfect profession, and they might be frustrated and resentful if they can't pursue it.

I recall the story of another smart student, one who was at the top of his eighth-grade class. When his favorite teacher asked him what he wanted to be when he grew up, he said a lawyer, though he hadn't really thought about it much. Unlike the rich, white college student, however, this poor, black boy was not encouraged to pursue law. His white teacher said, "That's no realistic goal for a nigger. You need to think about something you *can* be," suggesting carpentry as a more reasonable ambition. The boy resentfully abandoned the thought of being a lawyer, eventually taking up a life of crime instead. It wasn't until he went to prison that he started seeing how he had fulfilled society's low expectations of him instead of being true to himself. He read voraciously, found religion, and discovered he had a gift for persuading others with his passionate oratory, just like a prosecuting attorney. He became famous under the name Malcolm X for trying to change the society that told him he couldn't pursue the law.

The False Self can take many forms. Obviously being a successful lawyer is more acceptable to the wider society and more generously rewarded than being a street criminal, but from a spiritual perspective, these two young men were more similar than most people would think. Both were prompted to hide their

True Selves because of society's expectations of them, something most people do, though in less dramatic ways. Often we see this as simply being "realistic," the word Malcolm's teacher used. It's important to recognize that usually the people who encourage our False Selves think they have our best interests at heart. The college student's father thought he was doing what was best for his son by pushing him into a high-paying profession, just as Marcelle's friends thought that taking a job with health insurance would be best for her. Even Malcolm's teacher "probably meant well," as Malcolm himself put it, though he was obviously enforcing the social hierarchy, too. All of these people were reflecting two common assumptions of our culture, that safety and security are more important than authenticity, and that you can't have both—though many of the people interviewed for this book found both fulfillment and financial stability by being true to themselves.

Christian mystics like Thomas Merton describe the True Self as our link to God. Teresa of Avila, a Roman Catholic saint, went so far as to say that "one day of humble self-knowledge is better than a thousand days of prayer." Swiss psychologist Carl Jung believed that discovering our True Selves was one of our central purposes, especially in the second half of life, though he warned, "We must recognize that nothing is more difficult to bear with than oneself." This warning has been echoed by spiritual writers from Thomas Merton to the Dalai Lama. Knowing who we are may include admitting strengths we've been afraid to use, or it may include facing faults that our egos would rather keep hidden, even from ourselves. It may include the realization that we are not everything we have been told we are "supposed" to be by our families or communities. It may challenge us to change how we are living, something most of us resist. For instance, it would be difficult for the rich young man to admit to himself halfway through law school that he had made a mistake, even more difficult once he had a large mortgage, some kids in private school, and a wife accustomed to shopping at Nordstrom.

Sophie Williamson acknowledges that she resisted facing herself for most of her life. One night, when she was in her late fifties, she was cooking dinner when she heard a voice within her ask, "Do you want to know who you really are?" Sophie answered emphatically, "No!" Now seventy and more at peace with herself, she laughs at the memory. As she described in chapter 1, sharing her flashbacks of her abusive father with a therapist was one step to finding peace. Another key was paying attention to what was happening within her after she was diagnosed with leukemia in her early sixties. Through the years of treatment decisions, Sophie often had an inner sense of what her body needed, when to say no to a medication or take a day of rest. Eventually having a spontaneous remission, something her doctors said was impossible with her kind of cancer, she gradually came to trust her intuition, which has helped her to live with more clarity in other ways, as well.

"I'm very focused about what I want to do with the rest of my life," states Sophie, explaining that she feels called to work with children, both in her congregation's Sunday school and as a court-appointed special advocate, representing vulnerable children in legal cases. If she is asked to do something that does not have to do with helping children, she finds it easy to say no, which she did not always feel free to do before her cancer. As she explained in chapter 1, "All of life is easier" since she let go of her need to try to fix everything.

MIND GAMES

Although self-knowledge eventually brought Sophie much peace, it is striking that she resisted knowing herself for most of her life. It took two dramatic challenges—flashbacks from an abusive childhood and leukemia—to prompt her to look inward. Although the details are unique, her experience is not unusual. Many people find ways to avoid admitting what is really going on inside them. Denial is one of the most common games our egos play on us.

Sally Jergesen, who talked about her painful divorce in chapter 1, says that for years she ignored her intuition that she couldn't really trust her husband, especially when she saw him flirt with other women. Doubts would crop up, but she pushed them aside, like when he went to an out-of-town conference with a female colleague, and Sally felt uneasy. "I had this pretty strong tendency to trust what he told me verbally over what I observed with my own eyes or what I felt intuitively," she notes. Now a year after he left her and their young son, her ex-husband is living with the woman from the conference. Sally says, "I am in the process of learning to trust my intuition."

Denial is a common reason people don't change what they should, in their own lives and in the world around them. If we deny our intuition that we can't trust our husband, we won't have to confront him and risk losing the relationship. Likewise, if we deny our desire to be a teacher, we won't have to face disappointing our ambitious parents. If we deny our dissatisfaction with our job, we won't have to face the possibility of making a change. Ignoring our uncomfortable feelings may seem easier than facing the truth, but there is always a cost to denial.

Sometimes we ignore facing our own responsibilities by blaming others. I remember a newspaper photo of a pregnant woman smoking a cigarette as she looked out at some roadwork being done on her street. The caption said the woman was concerned about the effect the jackhammer noise might have on her unborn child. My daughter, who was ten at the time, saw the photo and asked with a laugh, "If she's so worried about her baby, why is she smoking?" Good question. Perhaps it was easier to blame the city for endangering her baby's health than to face the well-established fact that smoking while pregnant is unsafe. This does not mean that the mother's concern about the jackhammers was completely unwarranted—just that worrying about them might not have been the best use of her energy. Quitting smoking (difficult as that is) would surely be easier than getting her city to quit a roadwork project midway, though quitting cigarettes would require admitting the danger literally under her nose.

Sometimes an astute ten-year-old can see us more clearly than we can see ourselves, though when others challenge our denial, we often react with anger. When Hilary Beard's therapist first said she was work-addicted, Hilary got furious, believing her father was work-addicted, but not herself. Anger and denial are common responses when people don't want to acknowledge a difficult truth, which is why it is worth paying attention to what makes us really angry. Often it is because someone is challenging our False Selves, a painful process. This is one reason why sitting with emotions like anger and seeing what is behind them is so useful. Marcelle Martin's False Self did not want to see that there was anything wrong with her romantic relationship because seeing clearly would require her to speak up about the things that were bothering her. Denying what should be changed does not bring us serenity, however. It doesn't make us courageous, either.

My own experience of denial is that it makes me much more anxious than facing the problem does. During the time when I was starting to feel burned out in my activist job, I could see my job performance slipping in my decreasing fundraising numbers. I didn't want to admit my unhappiness, however, because I didn't want to disappoint my supervisor, whom I liked very much. In particular, I had made a two-year time commitment to that position, and I thought of myself as someone who didn't break commitments. So I buried my unhappiness and slogged along, despite many signs that things were not going well. When I finally got up the nerve to tell my supervisor that I wanted to leave, I burst into uncontrollable sobbing, releasing months of pent-up frustration. It was a huge relief. Soon afterward I realized that feeling trapped was making me unhappy more than the job was. Once I realized that I could quit, I didn't feel trapped anymore. Out of a new sense of freedom I decided to stay a few more months, fulfilling my original time commitment, before moving to Pendle Hill to pursue writing and deepen my spiritual life. It was a painful process, but I learned that facing my feelings and dealing with a problem are ultimately much easier than denial.

Matthew Cole sits at the kitchen table where he often says his morning prayers as he describes how he started getting drunk at age twelve. Twenty years and a lot of chaos later, a counselor suggested he might have a drinking problem. She handed him twenty questions formulated by Johns Hopkins University. "At the end, it says if you answer three or more of these yes, then you're probably an alcoholic," explains Matthew, who now uses the same questions as a sponsor for Alcoholics Anonymous. "I got eighteen out of twenty," he adds with a deep laugh. The survey helped break through his denial that his life was desperately out of control, prompting him to attend the meetings that helped him quit drinking.

It's no coincidence that breaking through denial is an important part of the same program that made the Serenity Prayer famous. A large part of accepting the things we cannot change is in breaking through denial. The Twelve Steps are designed to push people to face their addictions and the unpleasant aspects of themselves that lead to addictive behavior. Matthew notes that denial usually comes from fear. "We fear we're going to lose what we already have, or we fear that we're not going to get what we want," he explains. Although he says denial is still a challenge, years of following the Twelve Steps have helped whittle it down. "Denial doesn't happen as much and doesn't last as long," he says. "It's easier to face whatever the difficulty is. Usually it's something within me."

Alcoholics use the phrase "hitting bottom" to describe the crisis that shatters their denial and prompts them to get help. Many others have found crisis to play a similar role. For Sophie it was leukemia that helped her to get to know herself more deeply. For Marcelle it was a frightening pain in her heart. Sometimes cold, hard facts are enough. The twenty questions Matthew answered got his attention. Seeing our habits presented on paper can be an eye-opener, especially if the evidence is overwhelming, which is why diet experts tell people to keep track of their eating and financial experts tell them to keep track of their spending. Writing down what we eat or spend makes it more difficult to deny any patterns we would rather not acknowledge.

Elizabeth O'Connor, author of *Our Many Selves*, a religious approach to self-discovery, states, "Strangely enough we strengthen love in ourselves when we raise into full consciousness the shadow side of our lives. Conversely, when we keep negative feelings out of sight, they smother the love that seems to lie deeper and closer to the real self." Writing in the early 1970s, O'Connor pointed out that many people of her generation were rejecting the focus on sin by traditional religion and embracing more positive philosophies. She argued that we should not let the pendulum swing too far the other way, emphasizing only the positive aspects of ourselves and ignoring the difficult.

I agree that there is danger in focusing too much on one side or the other. While admitting our shortcomings is important, religions that encourage us to see only our faults keep us from discovering our gifts, which are also part of our True Selves. For Hilary Beard in chapter 1, acknowledging her creative gifts was an important part of becoming more authentic. Likewise for Marcelle, who over the years that she did not have a full-time job discovered that she had a deep spiritual understanding that could be helpful to others. Matthew observes that finding your strengths "lightens the burden tremendously. Even in the moments in my life when I was the most undesirable, I wasn't all bad, which is not only helpful for me in getting through looking at myself, it's also freed me to see that of God in others. It's given me more freedom, more love, more compassion for others."

Again, what you need to accept may depend on your background and conditioning. If you were raised by parents who cheered your every triumph and never criticized much, facing your weaknesses may be the difficult work you need to do. On the other hand, if your faults were always pointed out to you, acknowledging your strengths may be a necessary step to wholeness. Although it sounds more pleasant, admitting our strengths is not always easy, especially if they suggest we should change something about how we are living.

I remember once when I was in graduate school at Yale talking to a friend who was extremely intelligent, though not particularly tactful. He said he was surprised I was pursuing an academic career since I was so good at working with people. He thought I would be better at some people-oriented career, rather than research. At the time I was highly insulted, assuming he was questioning my intelligence. Years later—after I decided not to be a full-time academic—I realized that his comment had not been a put-down, as I had originally assumed. He was just honestly observing that I had strengths that were not being fully used in that environment. Hilary had a similar experience during her corporate career. Some of the older white men she worked with asked, "Why are you here?" initially prompting her to think they were questioning her ability to succeed and fit in as a black woman in an almost exclusively white male environment. After a while, however, she realized they were just observing the creative intelligence that made her feel out of sync in that setting. They were not insulting her, but seeing her.

Sometimes we twist other people's words or behavior, attributing meanings to them that were not intended. Marcelle recalls one time when she was teaching, and one of her students was hunched over in her chair with her arms crossed on her knees. Marcelle immediately read the student's body language as withdrawal from the class and assumed she was critical of Marcelle's teaching. "So I asked her afterward and she said, 'I have back pain, and that chair was really uncomfortable.' " Marcelle laughs at herself, something we could all do, though it's worth noting that the only reason she recognized her error was that she asked the woman what had been going on with her. Most of us don't ask for honest feedback from people we fear are critical of us, so we never get the chance to find out if our fears are baseless. (We also don't get to hear challenging feedback that might help us grow.) I've noticed that some of the best and most respected leaders I know are the ones who regularly ask for feedback. This has the obvious advantages of letting people learn from their mistakes and letting the people around them feel that their thoughts are valued, but seeking feedback has another, less apparent advantage: it helps to keep our projections in check.

Denying parts of ourselves often leads to what psychologists call *projection*, a phenomenon where we repress our own unacceptable or threatening feelings and then project them onto someone else. For example, after my mother's death, I wrote an essay about coming to terms with her racism and sent it to a member of my writers' group. She wrote back saying that she wanted to have tea to discuss it with me, which made me wonder if she hated the essay, found it offensive, thought I was a horrible person—or all three. For the months it took us to get together I'd feel a twinge of anxiety whenever I thought about it. Our subsequent lunch made it clear this was all in my mind. I had conflicted feelings about exposing my mother's racism and projected them onto my friend.

Sometimes we project qualities we can't face in ourselves onto people we think of as "other." I remember a cousin once being incredulous that I lived in a mixed-race neighborhood. "Aren't you going to get out of there?" he asked, as if I was picnicking in a war zone. I assured him that my part of the city was both friendly and safe, but he sounded skeptical. The funny thing was, my cousin had just gotten out of jail, was home on house arrest, and had called me to talk about his twenty-year-old daughter, who was on heroin and had recently begun robbing him. Yet this white man was afraid of my law-abiding black neighbors. He probably did not realize that *he* was the person *his* neighbors were afraid of. Maybe that realization would have prompted him to get help.

As soon as we feel the tendency to criticize someone else, we might ask ourselves what it is within us that the person has triggered. Although this practice takes courage, it would focus us on changing ourselves, which is easier than trying to change others. This is what Jesus was addressing when he asked, "Why do you see the speck that is in your brother's eye, but do not notice the log that is in your own eye?" You can be much more helpful to your neighbor if you remove the log in your own eye first. In fact, as long as you ignore the log in your eye, you can't see anything clearly. In other words, accepting yourself, faults included, is a prerequisite to wisdom.

Sometimes we have to deal with the judgments of other people, and these can be even harder to change than our own.

For Ro'Bin White Morton, a vivacious black woman from New Orleans, being told by her black classmates that she "sounded white" kept her quiet throughout elementary school. Now an outgoing artist dressed in bright colors, she recalls how painful it was to feel different from her peers. "I think sometimes when you're an artist, you're attacked because you're different," notes Ro'Bin. "People say things like, 'Who does she think she is?' or 'You think you're so wonderful.' " Ro'Bin admits that such comments have often made her feel numb. "What is the problem? That I love to laugh, love to have fun, love people?" Then one day Ro'Bin said to someone, "I can't help it if God made me great. If you have a problem with me, talk to God." Standing up for herself in that way was transformative. "I realized that people were not attacking me. They were attacking the God in me that they could not see. So I came to a revelation that it was spiritual warfare more than anything else." Dealing with rejection and resentment is still difficult for her, but it became easier when she started thinking of her strengths as a reflection of God.

Ro'Bin says her desire to please people sometimes keeps her from being true to herself. "Some of that comes from wanting to be polite," she observes. "The first twenty years of my life, I listened to my parents. My second twenty I gave to my children. And my third set of twenties—I find I've not yet come out of that subservient role, making sure that everyone else is all right, while I put my stuff on the back burner. So I'm trying to move out of that and do some things that I desire while I'm still here, especially after going through Hurricane Katrina." Surviving the storm and spending three days in the Superdome put the rest of her life in perspective. Ro'Bin shows me a children's book she has written about Katrina, an example of something she feels called to do, no matter what other people think.

AIDS TO SELF-KNOWLEDGE

An energetic woman who plays with the twists in her hair as she talks at her dining room table, Tracey Smith-Diggs has worked to define her own beliefs, having moved from church to church for many years. "One thing I never really believed that they tell you in some churches is that you are being selfish if you do things for yourself or get to know yourself," says Tracey, who has rejected many of the judgmental beliefs she grew up with. She recalls hearing one spiritual teacher say, "I am Spirit," an idea that struck her and stayed with her. "I don't think that I'm there yet," she says, "but really if you are made in the image of God, you are spiritual. We have to get back to knowing who that is. That's what I want. I really want to know Tracey, for real." She finds prayer and meditation helpful, as well as physical practices, such as yoga, massage, and walking in the woods. "I think it all works together, the mind, body, and spirit," she observes.

As Tracey points out, practices devoted to self-nurture or self-knowledge are sometimes seen as selfish, though there is a growing body of evidence that meditation can help people be healthier and more productive, as well as more self-aware. Meditation has been practiced for more than five thousand years, developed first in the Buddhist and Hindu traditions and now widely practiced in the West, as well. Although there are many forms of meditation, most aim to focus the attention of the mind on the present moment, so that anxious thoughts drop away. When the body is centered and the mind relatively quiet, people often find that thoughts or insights bubble up. We may take note of those distractions, and gently push them away. In some forms of meditation, like the one Marcelle described, staying with and uncovering our unconscious emotions may be the focus. In either case, breathing deeply helps calm us.

MEDITATION EXERCISE

Choose a quiet spot where you will not be interrupted for five minutes. Turn off phones and anything else that makes noise to get your attention. Find a comfortable place to sit. You may choose a chair with a straight back, like a kitchen chair, or a pillow on the floor. In either case, you should sit with your back erect and your head relaxed, but not slumped over. Let your hands rest comfortably on your legs, palms up. The idea is to become relaxed, but not so relaxed that you get sleepy.

Let your eyes close most of the way and take a deep breath. Exhale slowly, blowing out the stress and worries of the day. Allow your next breath to come at a natural pace, simply paying attention to each inhalation and exhalation. As you breathe in, think of the word "courage" as you feel your chest fill. As you exhale, repeat the word "serenity," as if you are exhaling all worry and stress. Repeat this with each breath for five minutes. The cycle of repeating "courage" and "serenity" should calm your mind and take it off every-day concerns that cause anxiety, making you feel both more peaceful and better able to function in the world.

As you meditate, other thoughts may come into your mind: the phone call you forgot to make, the embarrassing thing you said at work, or even how proud you are of yourself for meditating. Use the words "serenity" and "courage" to gently bring your attention back to the present moment. Don't feel bad if distractions continue to come. That is very normal. Just gently push the distractions aside. If you find the words themselves distracting, just focus on your breath. After you are finished meditating, you can jot down in a journal or meditation log how it went and what distractions arose for you. Sometimes the thoughts that come up in meditation are things that you need to deal with, but by meditating first, you will often be more clearheaded in handling what needs to be handled.

Start by trying this exercise five minutes per day. Over time, you can gradually increase the time you spend meditating. You may also want to experiment with different meditation techniques or styles. Find a local teacher or a book that will help you develop this skill. As many of the people interviewed for this book attest, regular meditation can help you know yourself and feel greater serenity. Thich Nhat Hanh points out that "breathing is the link between our body and our mind . . . when we breathe consciously we recover ourselves completely and encounter life in the present moment."

Buddhist monk and author Thich Nhat Hanh points out that conscious breathing can be practiced anywhere: "When you need to slow down and come back to yourself, you do not need to rush home to your meditation cushion or to a meditation center in order to practice conscious breathing. You can breathe anywhere, just sitting on your chair at the office or sitting in your automobile. Even if you are at a shopping center filled with people or waiting in line at a bank, if you begin to feel depleted and need to return to yourself, you can practice conscious breathing and smiling just standing there." Hanh teaches that this helps us to be more aware of our emotions and motivations, a practice Buddhists refer to as mindfulness.

In the Christian tradition, there has been a revival of the centuries-old practice of contemplative prayer, sometimes called Centering Prayer. While not everyone who practices meditation believes in God, in Centering Prayer there is an expectation that God is helping to reveal what we need to see. As Cistercian monk Thomas Keating writes in *Invitation to Love*, "The conscious resolution to change our values and behavior is not enough to alter the unconscious value systems of the false self and the behavior they engender," but he explains:

> The regular practice of contemplative prayer initiates a healing process that might be called the "divine therapy." The level of deep rest accessed during the prayer periods loosens up the hardpan around the emotional weeds stored in the unconscious, of which the body seems to be the warehouse. The psyche begins to evacuate spontaneously the undigested emotional material of a lifetime, opening up new space for self-knowledge, freedom

of choice, and the discovery of the divine presence within. As a consequence, a growing trust in God, a bonding with the Divine Therapist, enables us to endure the process.

The purpose of this divine therapy is not just our own healing, but healing our relationship with God, which will in turn affect how we live in the world.

For Yvonne Thompson, knowing and healing herself has enabled her to be of service to many other people, though it was a long journey. A tall, imposing woman with a rich voice and a deep laugh, Yvonne has won numerous awards as an advocate for older adults with mental illness, especially depression, which she has struggled with for nearly seventy years. In her youth, she started drinking to cope with her depression, but after a few years, the drinking became addictive, turning her life upside down and making her depression worse. "I've been homeless," she admits. "I know what it is to eat out of garbage pails." For years she tried to change. "I changed the kind of whiskey I drank, I changed my companions, and none of that worked," she recalls. "I was finally given to see that nothing was going to work because I cannot drink successfully." Although she had never denied the existence of God altogether, she says she "didn't believe that he or she took a particular interest in folk." But attending a Twelve Step group, she saw lives change so dramatically, she became convinced that a spiritual power was helping them. Gradually the same transformation took root in her own life, too.

Yvonne began meditating at the suggestion of a Hindu friend: "That was another revelation. That really, really helped me to become more in tune with the universe," she notes, adding that she learned a lot about herself, too. Now nearly eighty, she explains, "Of course I know more about myself today than I did thirty years ago or forty years ago, but I'm still learning, I'm still learning." Over the years she's had to learn how to forgive herself for the mistakes she made as a result of her addiction and mental illness, and this in turn has made her more forgiving of other people. "I've learned that I can do the same thing that anybody else can do, given a particular set of circumstances."

As Yvonne notes, self-discovery is a lifelong process. Matthew Cole says he has been helped by reflecting every night on the questions recommended by Alcoholics Anonymous: "Were we resentful, selfish, dishonest, or afraid? Do we owe an apology? Have we kept something to ourselves that should be discussed with another person at once? Were we kind and loving toward all?" These questions help Matthew to be honest with himself. He compares it to clearing debris that gets in the way of him knowing himself and God, of being the person he wants to be. He points out that there are other lists of questions, called inventories in AA, which focus on different issues, such as money, fear, or sex. Matthew notes that the inventories from Alanon, the organization for those close to alcoholics, ask more questions that help a person see their positive qualities as well as their negative ones.

The people in our lives can often help us develop self-knowledge, reflecting our strengths and weaknesses to us like a mirror. We do not need to believe everything everyone tells us, but we should be open to the possibility that others see things about us that we don't. If a writing teacher says you're talented, listen. On the other hand, if your closest friend or your therapist thinks you have a drinking problem or an abusive marriage, listen to that, too, and ask yourself if they might be right. Matthew recalls his current AA sponsor, whom he describes as "very blunt." Recently Matthew was complaining about his ex-wife when his sponsor said, "Well, you picked her. It's just another demonstration that your picker is broke." At first Matthew was quiet, but then he had to laugh, realizing it was true. There are other people who are very honest with him, including people from his faith community, and that in turn helps Matthew stay honest with himself.

No one can be more blunt than young children, which is one of the reasons parenting can be such a rich spiritual path. My own two have a charming way of pointing out my flaws and inconsistencies, saying things like, "If you don't want us to yell at each other, then you shouldn't yell at us," or, "You don't want us to spend too much time on the computer, but you check your e-mail all the time." While I'm not always grateful in the moment for such insight, I do know that motherhood has taught me more about myself than nearly anything else. Because I decided to stay home with my children when they were young, I was stripped of the crutches I had used to define myself—job, volunteer activities, even youthful figure. Sitting around home with baby drool on all my clothes made me wonder who I was in a deeper way. Losing my patience with the tenth game of Candy Land illuminated the parts of me that aren't very serene. Because young children live so in the present moment, caring for them can be an extended course in mindfulness.

I'm not sure how much is motherhood and how much is getting older, but since having children I've become much more aware of my body as a tool to excavate what is going on within me. Often heartburn or tight shoulders help me realize that I am under too much stress, just as a pain in her heart helped Marcelle realize that there was something wrong with her relationship. A few of the other people I interviewed shared similar examples. For Sharon Gunther, paying attention to her body has often helped her make decisions: "Do my body and spirit feel expanded and alive, or contracted and less alive?" asks Sharon. "I think I've used that at many points in my life, even as a young person."

A fifty-seven-year-old photographer with rosy cheeks and brown eyes, Sharon explains that her determination to nurture her spirit comes partly from the experience of having her mother enter a mental hospital when she was three and a half. "Coming from a really challenged home, I needed to have a lot of trust in myself. I learned what makes me happy and how to use my body as a spiritual clue for how I feel." This helped in the first major decision of her life, when in sixth grade a popular teacher offered to adopt Sharon. "Everybody wanted to be with this teacher," she explains. The teacher took the students on field trips and invited the quartet Sharon sang in to her beautiful home. In contrast, Sharon lived in a "poor little plain house" with her two brothers and their father, who was struggling to raise them. Her father said, "Well, she can give you a great education. She's got this beautiful home. She's wealthy. She and her husband could care for you in ways that I can't." But even at twelve, Sharon knew that it would be the wrong decision. "I said to my father, 'I cannot go and live with her. She has glass tables all through her house.'" She felt in her bones—as we say—that she would never feel relaxed in her teacher's house. "Now, that doesn't mean it wasn't difficult to stay at home with my dad and my brothers," adds Sharon, who points out that by society's standards, living with the popular, rich teacher was the logical thing to do. "People would say, 'Are you crazy?' But I think even then I was choosing the kind of values that were unquantifiable."

Sharon gives a more recent example of wisdom coming through her body. She had planned to skip an important meeting of her faith community to have dinner with a friend, partly because she was very angry with her congregation, particularly with a community leader who had been a good friend for many years. That afternoon, however, Sharon started to feel physically ill at the thought of missing the meeting. "The sickness was telling me if I didn't go and speak I was going to hold this poison forever," she recalls. As soon as she canceled her dinner plans, she felt physically better. Going to the meeting and speaking honestly took courage, but Sharon recalls, "I left feeling liberated." Two days later, when they ran into each other at a prayer gathering, the community leader from whom she had felt estranged apologized to her, and they began healing their relationship, which seemed to be an affirmation that it was right for her to have gone to the meeting.

Many people ignore their inner guidance when they can't see a logical justification for it, but Grace Potts believes that is a mistake. Grace learned to trust her intuition through twenty years of nursing, first in the ICU and now as a newly certified nurse midwife. She says that along with considering her medical training and her evaluation of the patient, she also tries to leave space for her "sixth sense." For example, recently she had a patient scheduled to have labor induced on Friday, but when a space opened on the schedule on Wednesday, Grace felt led to move up her

Friday patient. She did so without consulting the doctors who have to supervise her first hundred deliveries, and later learned that the two doctors she usually works with were both unavailable on Friday anyway. "That was the delivery where the cord came off in my hand," she recalls, describing one of her scariest deliveries to date. "The other doctor in town who would have been backing me up gets hyper and flipped out," she explains. "It would have been a disaster. But why did I even think that way? Why move it?" She says she wouldn't normally do such a thing, but working in the ICU for five years taught her to always trust her sixth sense, like when you have a feeling to just go back and double-check a patient. "You can be careless and not pay attention to that sixth sense, and it always gets you," she concludes.

Just as paying attention to our bodies and intuition can help us tap unconscious wisdom, so, too, can paying attention to our dreams. Although Marcelle says there are some dreams that seem to bring spiritual guidance from God, those are relatively rare. Most dreams really show us what is happening inside us. "Whatever the characters are, they are reflecting an inner drama," she says, echoing Carl Jung's explanation of dreams. Paying attention to dreams, she says, is "like looking in a mirror to see what's happening. It's not that you can take a dream at face value necessarily," she cautions. "If you take a dream too literally, you can get in trouble. They are really more metaphorical and symbolic, so it takes some working with them, living with them, to get the understanding. But it's a really good way of getting instant feedback about what the inner life is like." In order to observe how her inner life is unfolding, Marcelle keeps a dream journal by her bed to record her dreams as soon as she wakes.

While I agree with Marcelle that most dreams are metaphoric, occasionally people have a dream that helps clarify what they should accept or change in their lives. This was true for Hilary Beard, who early in her writing career was asked to co-author a memoir with Lisa Price, who had become a successful entrepreneur by listening to her intuition and valuing her unique gifts. "She trained me to listen to myself," says Hilary, "because I had never in my whole life known a single person who listened to themselves when it meant pursuing a path that was not the social norm." One of the ways Lisa's intuition worked was that Oprah came to her in dreams and told her to do something. "It's always something really ridiculous, but then it works," explains Hilary. While Lisa was visiting to proofread the book, Hilary had her own Oprah dream. "In my dream, Oprah told me I think too small about myself," recalls Hilary, explaining that every time she had an idea in the dream, Oprah said, " 'Hilary, that's a great idea, but it's too small for you.' She tells me I am capable of doing work that touches tremendous numbers of people, but not if I keep thinking small because I'm scared financially."

After the dream, Hilary went walking in the woods, a practice that helps her to stay spiritually grounded. She thanked God for the chance to write the book with Lisa and prayed about what would come next. "So I'm saying to God, 'Maybe I could work with someone who has some higher understanding that the world needs but who wouldn't be inclined to write it. I can help them write it and learn from them, but the book could help the world. Maybe that could be part of my purpose." Remembering the Oprah dream, she wondered how to make her idea bigger, and the thought came to work with a celebrity. "Ugh, not celebrity for the sake of celebrity," thought Hilary, "but maybe celebrity as a reflection of someone's excellence, their mastery of something, or their craftsmanship. It would be great to work with someone like that." She thought of tennis champions Venus and Serena Williams, whom Hilary had long admired, though they seemed too young to write a memoir. "A month later," recalls Hilary, "the phone rings and somebody I don't know calls me up and asks me if I'd like to work on a book about values for teenagers with Venus and Serena. So that's how I learned to listen to myself. That's how I got on purpose. That's how all this happened," she says, referring to the succession of book deals that followed.

As Marcelle cautioned, not every dream provides a road map that can be followed literally, but in Hilary's case, listening within gave her valuable insight that helped her to find her purpose, or to get in her lane, as she puts it. The next chapter explores the role inward listening plays in seeking divine wisdom and some tools for discerning when to accept things and when to work to change them.

Queries

Do you want to know who you really are? If not, what are you afraid of?

What do you know so far about your True Self?

Is it harder for you to accept the good in yourself or the bad?

How do the people in your life help you see who you are?

How do the expectations of people in your life prompt you to hide who you are?

When are some times you have projected onto someone else?

When is a time you overcame denial? What helped you?

What helps you to get in touch with your feelings and intuition?

Three

SEEKING DIVINE WISDOM

Hollister Knowlton grew up loving the earth, from the pristine lake in the Adirondack Mountains where her family had a summer cottage to the anthill in the front yard of her suburban Connecticut home. "From age six or so I remember having this reverence for nature," says Hollister, who is now in her late fifties with short brown hair speckled with gray. She recalls that as a young child, moving from the wilderness to the suburbs each fall, she felt troubled by the way human beings were destroying the natural world. Studying biology in college during the early years of the environmental movement increased "this sense of needing to save the world, but not knowing how and being overwhelmed by it." She decided that teaching high school biology would be her way to work for the earth, but her first two teaching jobs made her feel inadequate and depressed. "At that point I thought, 'Maybe I'm not capable of changing anything.'"

The depression persisted, along with a feeling that she should be doing more. It took many years for her to find her purpose—which she now describes as working "to transform the human-earth relationship."

Hollister observes that many of the blessings in her life have come from serendipity, like meeting a person who tells her about a new job. It was through a series of such incidents that she ended up working for an environmental advocacy organization where she began to understand how the American dream of a large house in the suburbs was hurting the environment and how zoning rules that separated housing from schools and stores made Americans dependent on their automobiles. The more she learned about how cars were contributing to global climate change, the more she wanted to give up hers. To make this possible, she saved money to purchase a tiny house in a city neighborhood where banks, groceries, and public transportation were all within easy walking distance. Six months after she moved, her car was stolen. "My reaction was funny," she recalls. "It was not anger, it was more, 'Oh yeah, I did say I was going to get rid of it. I guess the powers that be were listening and are making me live up to my promise.' "

Another coincidence occurred one day as she canoed with her future sister-in-law Suzie, who knew that Hollister had also cut animal products out of her diet to reduce her environmental impact. When Hollister mentioned that she had never found a community of kindred spirits, Suzie said, "I think you're a Quaker" because she knew that Quakers tried to live their principles. That intrigued Hollister, so a few months later she got up the courage to visit the local Quaker meeting. "I felt I had come home," she recalls. "Finding Quakerism transformed my life. I just marvel at how different my life is now from back in the seventies, when I just cried all the time, 'What can I do? What can I do?' "

Quakers gave Hollister plenty to do. First she heard an announcement for a regional Quaker environmental group. "I remember my heart just leaping and thinking, 'Maybe that's why I've found this place!' " Volunteering with that group led her to work with a national Quaker organization that was advocating for a different relationship between humans and the earth. For the first time, she felt she was really part of a community, working with others who shared her values. "Approaching this whole question of ecological sustainability from a faith-based perspective had a power to it that all of my work in teaching or public policy lacked," she explains. Especially after the terrorist attacks of September 11, 2001, she began to see sustainability issues as deeply connected to the global distribution of wealth and the U.S. dependence on the oil-rich Middle East. "I not only felt this sense of urgency about what I wanted to do, but I felt the irrelevance of my nine-to-nine job," she recalls, noting that by that point she was working long hours for a different nonprofit whose mission was less directly connected to her own.

Hollister negotiated a reduction in her paid hours and figured out how to live off less money. The more time she gave to environmental work, the more opportunities were presented to her, including the chance to attend the World Summit on Sustainable Development in Johannesburg. After the summit, she was able to play a new role, connecting people from different countries who were building sustainable communities. At a subsequent gathering in Colorado, Hollister made another such connection and thought, "Oh, God, this is my work!" The day she returned to her paid job, she was told that it was being eliminated, and her employer was offering her full retirement, severance, and benefits. "Again, I didn't have the courage to do it on my own," she admits. "But that was an answer to my prayers."

Near the end of our interview I observe, "So two of the best things that ever happened to you were getting your car stolen and getting fired?" She laughs heartily and says, "Absolutely!" (Though she quickly clarifies that she wasn't actually fired; her part-time position was eliminated.) "Often something had to intervene to nudge me along," she notes. Now a national leader of Quaker Earthcare Witness, Hollister is often asked to lead workshops and speak on sustainability. She wonders, "All the tiny little threads that had to come together to bring me here, were those by chance? Being led by the Spirit? I don't know." She says when Mother Teresa was trying to discern whether she should become a nun, a priest told her, "You'll know by your joy." "I guess that's what I feel now," she concludes.

You'll Know by Your Joy

When scholar of mythology and comparative religion Joseph Campbell popularized the phrase "follow your bliss," he did not mean bliss in a hedonistic sense, but the deep joy you feel when you've found your path. People use various terms for this experience, depending on their concepts of God. Quakers use the term "leading" for an inward pull that we believe has a divine source. Many use the word "calling" and think of it as "God's will," while others use less theistic phrases, like "getting in your lane" to express the idea that we each have a given purpose. Spiritual teacher Marcelle Martin says, "People say the will of God, but I think of it more as God's loving design." While getting in sync with this loving design does not mean that you will be giddy with joy every minute of the day, finding your purpose often brings both serenity and courage, not to mention clarity about what you should try to change and what you should just let go of and accept.

So how do you know where your lane is? How do you know if you are on track? A starting point is to know yourself and what your strengths are, as well as the ways you are prone to fooling yourself. The practices described in the last chapter help you to know not only who you are, but also what you might be called to do. Hilary Beard described it as learning to listen to herself, which, as she pointed out, many people do not do, though it is a practice encouraged by many spiritual traditions. If you accept the idea that there is a source of divine wisdom in the universe, and that you are connected to that Source, then it makes sense that listening within is crucial to accessing wisdom.

Although Hollister emphasizes the times something nudged her along, equally important were the times she had an inner affirmation that she was on the right track. She remembers her heart leaping and feeling she had come home when she found the Quaker meeting. Later, she remembers thinking, "Oh, God, this is my work!" after connecting people concerned with sustainability from different parts of the world. That inner affirmation helped her to stay serene days later when her paid work was eliminated. Even more important, she paid attention to her deep and persistent concern about the environment, which did not go away, even when she was doing something else. Although it took many years for her to find the exact work that has brought her joy, the seeds of her calling were planted in childhood.

Written by a group of Episcopalians who searched through scripture and spiritual autobiographies for patterns, the book *Listening Hearts: Discerning Call in Community* offers a summary of the many ways people can experience divine guidance:

> A call may come as a gradual dawning of God's purpose for our lives. It can involve an accelerating sense of inner direction. It can emerge through a gnawing feeling that we need to do a specific thing. On occasion, it can burst forth as a sudden awareness of a path that God would have us take. Call may be emphatic and unmistakable, or it may be obscure and subtle. In whatever way call is experienced, through the centuries God has chosen to speak to us and bids us to listen.

As *Listening Hearts* points out, we may each experience call differently or have different experiences at different times. Sometimes our inner guidance points us toward something outward, like a new career or new volunteer work. Other times our guidance is about our inner work, like cultivating serenity or courage. Sometimes God leads us to accept our circumstances, and at other times to change them.

Scripture is a primary source of spiritual guidance in many religions. The scriptures themselves tell of human encounters with the Holy, including dreams, visions, even experiences of hearing God's voice. In the Psalms, God promises, "I will instruct you and teach you the way you should go; I will counsel you with my eye upon you." Still, some fear it is arrogant to think that we, too, can hear from God directly, though it has been the experience of many, from mystics and saints to ordinary people like Ro'Bin White Morton.

A survivor of Hurricane Katrina, Ro'Bin feels God has saved her life several times over the years. A tall woman who loves bright colors and New Orleans music, she speaks quietly when describing the day many years ago when she was being choked by her then-husband. "I knew I was dying, 'cause he was choking the breath out of me," she recalls. "He was saying, 'I love you.' Then I heard God speak to me, and God said, 'I love you more.' " At that moment the breath came back into her body. As soon as her husband went out, Ro'Bin took her children and left for good.

A few years later, Ro'Bin had another experience of hearing God directly. This time the message brought her serenity. During this period she was a private tutor for the state, working in an after-school program, and dancing as part of a New Orleans documentary. One day she was rushing around her house, feeling anxious about all she had to do, when her body just stopped. "It was like my feet stuck, and I could hear the Lord speak to me, and He said, 'Stand still and know that I am God.' All of a sudden, my whole body calmed down. I stopped rushing, and I went on with the rest of my day, and my life started to change." Ro'Bin says after that incident she began to let go of her anxiousness. As her trust in life grew, good things started coming to her, including a loving relationship with the man she describes as "the love of my life," her new husband, W. B. Morton.

EILEEN FLANAGAN

When people tell me that they have heard something as clear as a voice, most often the message was deeply reassuring, bringing a sense of serenity in a time of turmoil. This was Sophie Williamson's experience. When she was first diagnosed with lymphocytic leukemia, she took the news calmly, although her grown daughters did not. After a few weeks of dealing with their anxiety and the many treatment decisions that were coming at her, Sophie herself started to feel overwhelmed. Then one afternoon, looking out the kitchen window, she saw a beautiful buck standing in her garden, only four feet from the window. She's always felt a deep connection to animals, and as she stood watching the buck in wonder, she heard a voice tell her everything would be all right. "This is so weird," she thought at first, but then she relaxed and trusted the message. Through the following years of her illness, she was able to face each stage with remarkable serenity, learning to trust the wisdom of her body.

There are many voices we can hear inside ourselves: our insecurities and fears; the justifications of our egos; the values of our culture; and the pressures of parents or others close to us, for starters. There are some voices people hear that may require professional help. So how did Ro'Bin know that it was God she was hearing? Couldn't Sophie have been practicing wishful thinking? These are legitimate questions. While many religions recognize that we can hear divine guidance, most also caution that not every voice in our heads is from a sacred source. Jesuit founder Saint Ignatius warned about our tendency to be influenced by spirits that are not the Holy Spirit. For this reason he wrote about "discernment of spirits," sifting through all the voices we hear to determine the source of an impulse. One clue, Ignatius said, was that only God could bring real joy.

In the Christian tradition, one way to test our discernment is to check it against the "fruit of the Spirit" listed in Paul's letter to the Galatians: "love, joy, peace, patience, kindness, goodness, faithfulness, gentleness, self-control." If the guidance we hear leads to these qualities, it is much more likely to be trustworthy. For example, the voice Ro'Bin heard led to more joy and peace in her life as well as to a much deeper understanding of the word "love." The voice Sophie heard after her diagnosis brought her a deep and lasting sense of peace and patience with her illness. In neither case did the voice prompt them to act in ways that were rash or selfish.

Although inward listening has been the subject of much of my writing and teaching, I have a knee-jerk suspicion of anyone who is *sure* they know what God wants—especially if they're sure God wants the same things they want and hates the same people they hate. We need only look at those who kill others in God's name to realize how dangerous arrogance in this realm can be. Any of us can be easily fooled by the less holy impulses within us, as Eileen Smith admits. A Sister of Saint Joseph for more than thirty years before she left to become a layperson, Eileen explains, "I'm a strong believer in intuition, and trusting it, and following it. I feel like it has guided me well in my life. Even if it's led to a failure, I still believe that it's been successful because it leads you to the next step. It really is the spirit of God, but you can't be glib about it, either. You can't just baptize everything and say, 'Oh, this is God's work,' because it's not true. You have to test it. You have to know yourself." In her early sixties with short gray hair and abundant energy, she admits that she has a strong will and sometimes tries to "force the round peg into the square hole" to get what she wants. She adds that discernment involves recognizing those impulses within yourself that are not from God. "It's just knowing what is operative without judging," she says.

Sharon Gunther, who discussed the wisdom she receives through her body in the last chapter, is aware of her own vulnerability. "I get misaligned when I'm too busy and I don't have my alone time with Spirit," she notes. During those times she feels her decisions come "out of a scarcity place," referring to the fear that there will not be enough, whether that means enough love, enough time, or enough money. She tries not to make major decisions when she is feeling this anxiety. "Then I know that I need to pay more attention to my relationship with God. When I do, things are clearer." Making space for her relationship with Spirit is so important to Sharon that she limits her photography work to three days per week, so she has ample time for quiet. "I need to do what expands me and gives me life," she explains.

Sharon mentions several practices widely believed to support inward listening and discernment. First, she makes nurturing her relationship with the Divine a priority. People may do this in many different ways: reading scripture or other spiritual books, walking in nature, praying, meditating, fasting, communal worship, or service, to name a few. Sharon is an outgoing person for whom communal worship and community service are vital, though she notes she also needs time for solitude, which is hard to find when she is too busy. Excessive busyness can also lead to stress and anxiety, known to make inward listening more difficult. Sharon recognizes that sometimes she gets "misaligned" and that those are not good times for making decisions.

Many of the practices that help us learn to trust our inner guidance go against the grain of our culture, which values busyness and productivity. While many people say they would love to feel less hectic, few are willing to follow Sharon's lead and cut their work time (and therefore their incomes) to do it. Others are not paid enough per hour to make this possible, especially if they are also raising a family, a responsibility that, as I know all too well, makes it even more difficult to find quiet. Even when we do have moments of solitude, we often have the TV or the iPod filling our brain waves, making it hard for the nudges of the Spirit to get any airtime. In such a fast-paced media-saturated culture, we may start to expect that every problem can be resolved in a half-hour time slot, every message received as quickly as an e-mail.

Divine guidance is not always so rapid or clear. Many people experience it as more of a gradual dawning, like a sunrise rather than a lightning bolt. For this reason, most spiritual writers suggest allowing time for answers to unfold, rather than demanding an immediate solution. Quakers in particular often use waiting as a way to test a sense of call. We assume that if God is asking us to do something, the feeling will last, whereas if it is just a whim or an impulse it will pass with time. For example, Hollister Knowlton's feeling that she should work to save the earth lasted for years and kept coming back to her, although the exact wording she used to describe her work evolved over time. Her sense of call has also been tested by another common Quaker method, gathering a small group of wise people to listen to us when we are seeking clarity, a process described in chapter 7, "Finding Wisdom in Community." Often, when such a group senses that we are not yet clear, they will suggest we wait, knowing that if we are called to change something, the feeling will usually persist.

Waiting for clarity can be applied to many different aspects of our lives, not just our careers. Sarah Whitman recalls hearing that no one was volunteering to lead the religious education program for middle school at her congregation. The mother of a fifth-grader and a professional psychiatrist, Sarah started thinking that maybe she should volunteer, but was unsure. "Do I know enough?" she wondered. "Am I cool enough to work with middle schoolers?" Sarah decided to listen inwardly before making the decision. "I feel I am only in the beginning stages of learning discernment," she explains, "but there were several clues I used to figure out what God's plan was for me. The idea of being involved with the middle school program returned to me repeatedly, and seemed to *come to* me, more so than my struggling intellectually over the pros and cons of the decision. I also had a growing sense of peace and excitement about doing the work, rather than increasing apprehension or concerns about it."

Teaching middle school gradually started to feel inevitable. "It was a sense, deep down, that I was called to do this, but that God would be patient while I went through my human muddlings, until I accepted." Sarah noticed that she had been given several experiences the previous year that had prepared her to teach. "I felt in awe of the intricacies of God's plans," she recalls. Now, after several months in her new role, she feels that many gifts have come to her as a result. "I have felt that *I* am not developing these lessons, but rather that they are being given to me," says

Sarah, who has made it a spiritual practice to listen each week for guidance about what she should do with the children. This sense of being a channel, continually open to divine guidance, has been the most profound blessing. "Over the last few years, I have been looking for ways to increase my sense of connection to God during the week," she explains. "I have tried midweek worship, different types of meditation, and a spiritual companions group, yet none of these has felt quite right. So in an unexpected calling, I have found an answer to a deep desire."

DISCERNMENT EXERCISE

Set aside some time for quiet in a peaceful place. You may want to do this exercise in your home or in a place of natural beauty, like a garden, park, or retreat center. You may want to write your answers in your journal, or just sit in a meditative pose and let the answers bubble up from your gut, rather than letting your head rush in with a logical answer.

Recall Hollister Knowlton's experience of saying, "Oh, God, this is my work!" Is there something you feel that way about now? (It may or may not be your paid work. For example, caring for a family may be a calling.) If so, what is it, and what makes it feel right? Did clarity about this calling come quickly, or gradually over time? Does this calling bring you joy and meet the needs of others simultaneously? Are you devoting an appropriate amount of time to this work?

If you have never experienced a sense of calling, think about moments when you have felt as if you were fully alive, using your unique gifts. What do these moments have in common? What keeps you from living this way more often? What fears would you need to move past in order to "follow your bliss"? Have you ever ignored an inner sense of what you should be doing? If so, what was the result?

After giving time to each of these questions, close by asking God or your Higher Power or the Universe to guide you in finding or staying on your path.

Often spiritual guidance brings an unexpected solution to a problem, and often that solution benefits others as well as ourselves. Author and Presbyterian minister Frederick Buechner offers this guideline: "The place God calls you to is the place where your deep gladness and the world's deep hunger meet." This summary rings true to my observation that people who have found their deep gladness usually are having some positive impact on other people. This does not mean we should be consumed by the world's deep hunger, or assume that we should respond to every need we see. As Ro'Bin White Morton pointed out in chapter 2, she sometimes puts her joy on hold because she was conditioned to take care of others first. There are some things that should be changed, only not by us. Part of wisdom is figuring out which problems are ours to solve.

Professor David Watt, who described having his image of God expanded in chapter 1, has been thinking about this aspect of wisdom: "One of the things that I've thought in the last ten years working with spiritual directors is that a lot of one's job is just to stay in one's own lane. It's a football metaphor. There's a kickoff. Everyone has a lane they need to stay in, and in order for the kickoff to be covered successfully, you don't go running around wildly. You just stay in your lane. So that means not trying to be responsible for everything, but just trying to be responsible for the cards you've been dealt." One way to see if you're in your lane is to pay attention to what opportunities you've been given and to see if they correspond to what your inner guidance is telling you. Like Hollister, as well as Eileen Smith, we may find that the inner and outer signs match when we are in our lane.

Matching the Inward and Outward Signs

Eileen Smith was a sister of Saint Joseph, working at a parish in an urban neighborhood when she started to feel led to start a non-profit to serve poor people in the community. The parish had a meal program that put her face-to-face with the need. "When you sit with people at a table and you break bread, you just can't stop there," she explains. "As we were having these meals every weekend, we started hearing stories from people about their health, their kids, their addiction, their mental health, their loneliness, their desperation." At the same time, she started hearing offers of help from the parish's mostly middle-class parishioners. "You know, Eileen, I could help you start a legal center," said a lawyer. Someone else said, "What about a summer camp for the kids?" Eileen mimics an amazed look. "There were people who came forward and stood with us and really made it work," she recalls.

Eileen felt that starting a nonprofit to serve a greater range of community needs was the right thing to do, especially since the parish was feeling financially strained by the meal program and wanted it to get its own funding source. The number of volunteers who came forward encouraged Eileen. Still, she knew they needed money and staff to stabilize the effort because she didn't want to start something and then let people down. "You really do have to keep showing up," she notes. At first the funding did not come as easily as the volunteers. "It had some false starts in the beginning where things didn't really pan out. I had to keep going back to it," she recalls. Today Eileen is the executive director of Face to Face, a freestanding nonprofit with a dining room, a legal center, a health center, an after-school program, a summer camp, and an arts program. Although they serve several hundred people per week, Eileen says the giving is mutual. "That's why we are called Face to Face," she explains. "There is something in the encounter that is mutually life-affirming. You just know there is a meeting of the God in all of us. I live by that," she concludes.

There are many signs that Eileen discerned her call correctly. It has resulted in several of the "fruits of the Spirit," and benefits others as well as herself. The work has had a sense of rightness that has lasted over time, now more than twelve years since the organization's founding. Furthermore, circumstances fell into place that supported what she was doing. The universe encouraged her by sending the help she needed. Although there were points when she had to swim harder than others, she seemed to be swimming in the direction of the current, to paraphrase Hilary Beard's Baptist minister from chapter 1. Quakers call this "way opening" and use it as one test of whether we are in our lane.

In my experience, way opening is a gift, though it often involves a combination of human and divine action, like a supermarket door that swings open only after you step toward it.

When I was still relatively new to Quakerism, I decided to become a resident student at a spiritual study center called Pendle Hill. As soon as I read the beautiful brochure, I *knew* this was where I was supposed to be. I told everyone I was going there before my application was even accepted. The only stumbling block was money. Even one semester cost more than my meager savings. I had a sense that the money would work out, and it did—but only after I asked everyone I met there about possible funding sources. One Pendle Hill teacher mentioned a private fund that gave grants to people the grantors believed were following God's leading, so I sent them a letter explaining why I felt led to go to Pendle Hill. I had already moved there when I got their response, which said that they try to listen for God's guidance when making grants and that they had felt led to offer me twice the amount of money I had requested so that I could stay a second semester. For me, it was a dramatic example of way opening; the letter affirming my decision to pursue this spiritual path was almost as meaningful as the money.

Of course it's easy to believe God is behind it when someone gives you money or a book contract. It's harder to know what God is up to when the way does *not* open. These are moments when you may be challenged to accept uncertainty before the next steps become clear. After my two semesters as a student at Pendle Hill, I stayed on as a staff member (another case of way opening), but when I later felt ready to move on and pursue writing full-time, the way got a little fuzzy. A friend and I planned to rent a beautiful house in the Pennsylvania mountains where we could both write. The plan seemed perfect until I learned that the current residents of the house had a problem. Rain was slowing construction on their new home, so they would be staying in my dream house a bit longer—weeks, maybe months. With nowhere to go in the interim, I stayed at Pendle Hill, snapping at any well-meaning community member who asked me how my plans were coming along. I was not exactly an exemplar of serenity. My attitude was so bad that I decided not to bother getting to know the new group of students who were arriving. I had mentally checked out already. Then one morning I felt my resistance melt away during meditation. I finally accepted that I was part of the community for another semester and immediately started noticing what a nice group of students had arrived—including the man who eventually became my husband.

I've come to trust that when things don't look like they are going well, it's often because God has something better in store for me than what I had in mind. Usually I have to stop whining and accept whatever is before I can appreciate what could be. As Mother Superior said in *The Sound of Music*, "Whenever God closes a door, somewhere He opens a window." The thing is, you won't notice the window until you stop banging on the door. Still, there are times when you are meant to bang on the door because the way can't open until you put a little more muscle into it. So how do you know the difference between going with the flow and letting yourself drown? That is one of the main challenges of the wisdom to know the difference. One answer is to see if what is flowing within you matches the direction of the current around you. You have to pay attention to your joy and to the cards you are being dealt.

One of Hal Taussig's joys has been travel, which he discovered riding trains throughout the West with his father's award-winning cattle herd. Another joy has been simple living, which he discovered in the years after his own cattle business went bankrupt from a sterile bull. Although initially crushed by the bankruptcy, Hal began to question society's emphasis on acquiring material wealth and learned to enjoy reading magazines in the library rather than subscribing to them and riding a bike to work, something he still does today at the age of eighty-three. "I embraced failure," he says with a twinkle in his eye. "I didn't ever feel desperate."

After several years as a teacher, Hal had the idea to help teachers and others on a tight budget who wanted to travel to Europe and experience more of the local culture than they would on an expensive trip. When he first founded Untours—an unconventional travel agency that arranges for travelers to stay in apartments, rather than fancy hotels—Hal made calls from a phone booth because he couldn't afford a phone. "Then the money started coming, so I had a problem," says Hal, who by then had realized that he liked living free of property or investments. The first year his business made a profit, Hal gave a refund to his puzzled customers. Next he shared the profits with his employees, but it created friction when employees with seniority felt they deserved a greater share than newer hires. "These are middle-class people with college degrees I'm giving the money to," he realized. "If I'm going to give my money away, I should give it to the poor. So that's when I thought of starting the nonprofit."

Now in its fourteenth year, Untours Foundation has provided more than $5 million in low-interest loans to projects that provide opportunities for people who are poor. One of its micro-loans helped to build a vibrant crafts fair in Hanoi. Another helped urban American women move off welfare by launching a business cooperative that provides home health care services. Instead of pride in his good works, Hal exudes humility and gratitude. Although he has not saved anything for his old age and lives in a small house that he and his wife do not own, Hal says living with vulnerability is part of life and keeps him feeling close to poor people. "I'm still open to failure," he explains. "The more I can give myself to God to control my life, the more freedom I have."

There are many signs that Hal's early failures helped him become more authentic, more his True Self. He doesn't measure his life in possessions or portfolios, but in how much good he is doing. He doesn't feel anxious about his vulnerability, but trusting and grateful. A key to finding this serenity came from the realization he shared in chapter 1 that his real worth came from being a child of God. That insight helped him through experiences that could have been very frustrating if he had continued believing that his worth came from being a successful cattle rancher, like his father. Instead, losing his cattle herd led him to work that is both fulfilling and helpful to others (the work itself, as well as the profits from it). Similarly, the reason Hollister Knowlton was so sanguine about accepting a stolen car and a lost job, which many people would have found upsetting, was that those events helped her to live more authentically. They pushed her in a direction she already wanted to go. The flow of the outward current matched the direction of her inner current. Recognizing this made accepting what she could not change easy.

I've heard other people say that getting fired was a blessing that helped them to follow their inward guidance. This was true for Tracey Smith-Diggs. She had been running art and music therapy programs at a large university hospital for about ten years and was known as an advocate for patients. Two of the people she reported to, however, were very negative, making for a tense work environment. First Tracey tried to keep herself grounded, getting to work early to pray at her desk and light incense in her sunlit corner office. That helped, but eventually she realized she should leave and start her own business as a personal consultant. "I didn't have another job, so it was really a step in faith," she explains. She made the move, but after being on her own a little while she got scared of her financial vulnerability and went back to her old job. "It was horrible," Tracey recalls, laughing because this time she got fired. "I'd *never* gotten fired from a job, *ever*. But I think the Holy Spirit was like, 'I told you what to do!' The Holy Spirit will let you know, 'This door is closed.' "

"I've learned to trust the Holy Spirit," explains Tracey, who has worshipped with a wide variety of Christian denominations. Now in her forties, she's come to trust her own relationship with the Creator, rather than believing the creed of any one church. "It's amazing to me," says Tracey, whose consulting business has steadily grown since her firing. "I just put it out there, how much money I need to make, and slowly but surely it has built up. Everything I ask the Holy Spirit for just comes to pass if I stay on the path. I want to do these types of workshops; I get to do these types of workshops." Part of her work now is doing pregnancy prevention at an urban high school where the students desperately need positive adult role models. Tracey notes that if she had not been fired, she would probably have stayed in her old job for the money. "I wouldn't be able to do all that I'm doing now," she concludes.

Tracey's and Hollister's stories illustrate how inner and outer signs sometimes converge. Both were given new opportunities as they moved into the work they felt called to do. Way opened. The corollary is that way can also close, as it did on Tracey's university career. She took it as a sign that the Holy Spirit didn't want her working there because this matched what her inner guidance was already telling her. In fact, the outer sign of getting fired made it easier for her to follow the inner guidance she was resisting, just as for Hollister getting her car stolen helped her to be faithful. The important point here is that for each woman, the outer circumstances reflected her inner truth. Although Tracey might have been tempted to blame her boss for her firing, in these circumstances she couldn't do it. "She might not have been a nice person," says Tracey, "but there was something that I was supposed to do, and I was being disobedient to the Holy Spirit."

While Tracey and Hollister both accepted what they couldn't change pretty easily, it was much more difficult for Grace Potts, though she says she can see God's work in hindsight. All Grace ever wanted was to be a midwife and a mother, but when she was seventeen she was present at a cousin's difficult home birth with an inexperienced midwife, an event that scared Grace off midwifery for years. When she got the devastating news that she was infertile, she was grateful she had gone into Intensive Care nursing instead. "I went through ten years of anger about the infertility," she recalls. "I would have been bitter, bitter, bitter if I had been caring for pregnant women." She tried numerous fertility treatments and two surgeries to unblock her fallopian tubes. On the eve of her third surgery, Grace was at a work party and heard that her doctor had gone to the hospital to treat a thirteen-year-old who had just given birth. "I went home that night and sobbed and sobbed. Thirteen-year-olds can have babies! And all I ever wanted was to be a midwife and have babies and garden." She told her husband she felt suicidal, not knowing that the baby delivered that night would be offered to her for adoption. "So in the pit of my darkness, that was our baby. That was a prayer answered, there's no doubt," says Grace.

Grace really believes in the concept of way opening, though she understands how painful waiting for the way to open can be. She also understands the difficulty of figuring out how hard to try to make something happen. Even though she tried most of the fertility treatments available, she says, "I just had this feeling that if I wasn't meant to get pregnant, I wasn't meant to get pregnant." Now a nurse for twenty years, she says nursing has taught her the danger of trying to control too much. She appreciates modern medical technology, but believes "it's only a tool. It is extraordinarily dangerous in the wrong hands." She recalls an experience in the ICU years ago that taught her humility. A patient who was a Jehovah's Witness refused blood products because of his religious beliefs, and Grace felt angry that he would risk his life in that way. "Not long after, HIV came out, and I had to say to myself, 'Wow, I don't know. Maybe he would have gotten tainted blood.'"

Today Grace brings that humility to her new midwife practice, along with the medical skills she gained from working in the ICU. In hindsight, Grace feels that God was guiding her, both in the decision to delay midwifery training until after her infertility struggles, and in the decision to pursue midwifery after becoming a mother herself. "You don't know the big picture," she concludes. "You don't know it down the road. One thing does lead to another." Remembering that you don't know the big picture can be helpful when things don't work out the way you want or expect.

Why Doesn't God Fix It?

Surrounded by papers, awards, and pictures of her children, Celeste Zappala takes time out of her work running a social service agency to share a profound experience she had when her son Sherwood's National Guard unit was being deployed to Iraq. She was working in her garden, praying that some last-minute change would keep him from going to fight in a war she opposed. "God, let this cup pass," she said, echoing Jesus' prayer the night before his crucifixion. "Make something happen so that he doesn't have to go." The answer she heard was not comforting. "I had this overpowering sense of 'Who do you think you are that you don't have to feel the grief of the world?' That phrase was in my head, 'the grief of the world.' What would make me think that I wouldn't have to taste that? Why would it be just other people?" Celeste felt that whatever was going to happen was going to be very difficult, but she would get through it. When Sherwood was killed months later, she vowed to honor his memory by working to end the war. Since then she has modeled her peace work on Martin Luther King, Jr., who sought to speak to people's compassion rather than their hate.

Although Celeste is a deeply religious person, she struggles with the concept of God's will. "I don't think it's God's will that we have wars. I don't believe that it's God's will that we kill each other. I think that it is God's sorrow that we do those things. It is opposed to every moral teaching of the universe. So why doesn't God fix it? Because we have free will and conscience. God put that challenge in front of us." She says this doesn't necessarily mean that Sherwood's death was preordained, but that she was called to deal with that possibility with compassion, rather than with hate. "Things occur, and it's God's will that we use the best of ourselves in order to deal with the things that occur and stand up for God's morality, as we discern it."

Chris Ravndal, who taught prayer at Pendle Hill for many years, says that when he was young he asked God for yes-or-no answers, like should he do this or that. He got answers, he says, but now in his seventies, he feels there is a danger in asking God to make our decisions for us. Not only does it "make us vulnerable to influences that are not God," it can keep us from developing our own power of choice. "God gives us the tools and basic knowledge with which to build our structure rather than the architect's plan," he explains. "You must reach your own decision, keeping before you the basic principles and constantly seeking God's assistance in arriving at your decision." This builds in us the confidence and judgment to take responsibility for our own choices.

While we must accept that we do not completely control our destiny, we must also accept that we do have choices and, therefore, responsibility. While we don't totally control our health, we do choose every day whether to eat vegetables and exercise, decisions that have a profound impact on our health. We don't control other people, either, but we do choose whether to practice respect and honesty, which in turn impacts how others treat us. We certainly don't control the weather, but as individuals, we choose whether to heed a hurricane warning, and as a society, we choose whether to invest in levies or alternative fuels to slow global warming. As groundbreaking psychologist Rollo May paraphrased Nietzsche, "Though it is arrogance to say we are 'masters of our fate,' we are saved from the need to be the victims of it. We are indeed *co-creators of our fate*."

Malik Mubashshir converted to Islam after studying comparative religion at Harvard Divinity School. Now the head of a high school history department and interim imam of his mosque, he explains that there are many commonalities among Christianity, Judaism, and Islam, including a tension between divine power and human responsibility. "Here is a characteristic Islamic understanding of that," he begins. "Someone came to the prophet Mohammed and said, 'Oh, messenger of Allah, should I trust in God, or should I tie up my camel?' And the prophet said, 'Trust in God, *and* tie up your camel.' So you have to do both. Anything that is in your power, anything that is in your sphere of influence, you're responsible for that." He points out that Muslims often say *mashallah*, which means, "It has happened according to God's will," a view that can be very comforting when things do not go the way we wish. It can help us to let go and move on. On the other hand, he adds, "We are moral agents. We are decision makers. We have an effect on our families, on our classrooms, on our workplaces. So much rests on our heads. That's not comforting. It is uneasy, but I think it's a healthy uneasiness. That's the tension we have to live with."

The relationship between God and Moses is an important model of divine-human partnership in Judaism, Christianity, and Islam. Like many of us, Moses at first doubts that he could possibly be of use to God and tries to wiggle out of his mission with excuses about his powerlessness. Finally God convinces Moses that God will be with him and will give him the power he needs. Based on this reassurance, Moses does the hard work of gathering the Israelites, who are in slavery in Egypt. Although they are afraid and don't have time to let their bread rise, Moses leads them to the edge of the Red Sea, with the Egyptian army bearing down on them. Moses tells the people to be still, fear not, and trust in God. And God responds, "Why do you cry out to me? Tell the Israelites to just get going." As instructed, Moses stretches his hand over the sea, but it is God's power that drives the water back so the Israelites can pass to safety.

In *Be Still and Get Going*, Rabbi Alan Lew explains that when Moses says to be still, and God says to get going, God is not contradicting Moses, as it may first seem. The people have to let go of their fear and pull themselves together before they are capable of crossing the Red Sea. It is only when they accept their circumstances that the Jews can see what they must do next. "What the Torah seems to be hinting at here is something akin to the Taoist idea of *wu wei*, or nonaction," explains Lew, who has found many correlates between Judaism and eastern religions. Lew describes *wu wei* as "action in perfect alignment with the moment." He explains that God will fight for us, but we need to get our egos out of the way. In other words, we must accept our circumstances and then take the next necessary step.

The concept of *wu wei* comes from the ancient Chinese philosophy of Taoism. Although Taoism does not use God language, Lew's description of "action in perfect alignment with the moment" is compatible with the idea of a human-God partnership. It does not imply apathetic passivity, but going with the flow, working with the nature of things, being more efficient because we are not wasting energy on being anxious. In fact, *wu wei* could be described as swimming in the direction of the current, as Hilary Beard's minister put it. Many Westerners relate to Taoism's famous symbol of yin and yang, which illustrates the relationship between stillness and movement and the need for both. For example, relaxing and breathing help during childbirth, but at a certain point you need to push. It's not a contradiction. Breathing helps you push, just as trusting God helped the Jews cross the sea.

Melvin Metelits says that he had a "Red Sea moment" of his own ten years ago when he heard the doctor say, "You have cancer." Now in his seventies with a gray beard and gray hair framing his skullcap, or *kippah*, Melvin paraphrases author Rabbi Laurence Kushner: "There's a split second where you realize you've left the past, you'll never go back to it, and yet the future is uncertain. That's the Red Sea moment," explains Melvin. "When the doctor said, 'cancer,' I was at one of those moments where I knew that my past would not be the same, and my future was uncertain. So I cried. That was my response. I cried." He was sixty-three and newly returned to Judaism after having rejected religion for nearly fifty years.

From a comfortable couch in his book-filled living room, Melvin says that for most of his life he was not a person who accepted things with serenity, but his cancer pushed him to grow in new ways. "Emergencies are spiritual fodder," he notes. "Sometimes there's a wisdom that comes to you in a moment of crisis." Recalling his cancer, he says, "I had to have the serenity to know that I could not change what was, and the courage to proceed with the best treatment available to me." In a voice still raspy from the throat surgery that removed his cancer, Melvin explains that acceptance and action are both important in the Jewish tradition, which he has been studying intently for the past thirteen years. They are cyclical and interrelated, neither being an endpoint, particularly in the ancient, mystical tradition of Kabbalah. Pulling out a diagram of the "Tree of Life," Melvin points to two opposite circles labeled *Netzack* and *Hod*, explaining that they can both be translated as "victory," though *Netzack* represents a more active, outward energy, while *Hod* is the victory of appreciation and acceptance. "They are companions and opposites. For health, each one must contain elements of the other."

Although Melvin is now cancer free, his voice has never regained its former volume or strength. He notes, "Once I accepted that this was my voice, the next question was, 'So what do you do about it?' That's the cycle: the acceptance is merely the plateau from which you launch your next action in the world. Serenity becomes almost like a tool rather than a complete way of life." For Melvin, that next action was to become a *maggid*, which means a holy storyteller. Although his voice is raspy, he is able to captivate and teach his listeners with tales from the Hassidim, something he might not have found the courage to do if he had not first come to peace with his new voice.

Melvin points out that after God delivered the Jews, God didn't let Moses stay up on Mount Sinai, though that would have been most pleasant for Moses. God sent him back down the mountain and put him to work. "No matter how much serenity you have, there's always something more to do," says Melvin, who explains that spirituality is not just about healing ourselves. It is also about healing the world. "In Torah God says, 'Build me a *mishkon*, a temple, a holy place so that I may dwell among you.' We take that to mean, make the world God's temple. And you don't make the world God's temple only by meditation and individual spirituality. Spirituality in our Hassidic tradition reaches its highest form in doing in the world, not in meeting God. We meet God only for purposes of coming back down to do work."

Melvin's description rings true to my understanding of our relationship with the Divine. We seek to follow God's guidance, not only out of a sense of obedience, but also out of a sense that God needs us to do God's work in the world, to make the world God's temple, as it were. Sometimes it is through such work that we feel a profound sense of connection to a spiritual power greater than ourselves. As Rabbi Erin put it, we see a spark of the Divine in someone else, or see the Divine in us touch them. We have a sense of being used by God and of meeting God simultaneously.

Father Michael Doyle explains the philosophy of Sacred Heart parish, located amid desolate urban streets near a putrid New Jersey sewage treatment plant. "There is a basic principle that we follow that liturgy leads to justice," he says in the brogue of his native

Ireland, which he left nearly fifty years ago. "If you gather and celebrate the Eucharist, then there is a profound responsibility to apply that communal approach to life and to seek justice and fairness for people and to promote peace, so that it's not just talk or theology." Father Michael applies this philosophy by supporting the dignity of his neighbors. He observes that often opportunities come without his planning. Years ago, for example, one of his neighbors said that he was going to have to move because his landlady was selling his house. It turned out the landlady owed $600 in taxes and didn't have the cash. Father Michael decided to just buy the house and let the tenant pay him each month until the debt was repaid, at which point the tenant would own the house. "That was the beginning of the Heart of Camden housing program," he recalls. "I saw that if we had money, we could change renters into owners, and if you had owners, you'd have stability and neighborhood. But did I come up with the idea? No, the need was presented to me, and I responded to it."

More recently some parishioners had the idea to begin sponsoring plays focused on justice, war, and racism. "One thing poor people have is talent," says Father Michael, explaining that the plays have become another ministry that makes room for people's dignity. "I would never have thought of that," he admits, "but it is ministry." Now a donor has come forward to build a small theater on a vacant lot across from the church. "Sometimes things just come, and they are absolutely right," he notes. Although Father Michael believes that people should use the power they've been given to make a difference, he acknowledges that it is in partnership with God. Speaking of his role in leading mass, he says, "The lift to God is God's work. You can't lift people. Your job is to lead the ritual as authentically and as well as you can. Like a piece of music, do it as well as you can, and let it flow. If the spirit soars, that's God's work."

Recognizing that we cannot control everything can free us to pay attention to all that is in our domain. Although "the lift to God is God's work," as Father Michael put it, we can prepare ourselves to be the best channels possible. This begins with shifting our perspective, which after all is one of the things we have the power to change. As Buddhist scholar and teacher Reginald Ray explains, "The desire to change the world is a very good thing. However, if you don't work on yourself first, you'll bring all of your personal paranoia, arrogance, aggression, and preconceptions along, and you'll just get in a fight with whomever you're trying to change." Ray does not mean we have to be perfect before we can have an impact on anyone else, just that like Gandhi and many other great leaders, we have to begin with changing ourselves, the subject of the next chapter.

Queries

Are there times when you feel both joyful and of service to others?

Do you believe it is possible to hear Divine guidance?

Have you ever felt God guiding you? If so, how did you know it was God?

Have you ever felt a deep sense of peace or clarity come to you in a time of decision or difficulty?

Have you ever felt led to change a situation?

Have you ever ignored or denied your inner guidance? Why?

What fears do you have about following your inner guide?

If you were to translate the proverb "Trust in God, but tie up your camels" for your own life, what would it say?

Four

SHIFTING YOUR PERSPECTIVE

ill Brock realized as a child that he wanted to be a musician, an unusual goal for a boy in a small town where there seemed to be only two classes of people: factory workers and office workers. "Everyone around me besides my family said, 'You're nuts,' " recalls Will, noting that most people he knew just wanted to get a decent job with benefits. Now an established singer, composer, and keyboardist with recordings and a busy performance schedule, he notes that his hometown was a great place to grow up and develop a strong moral framework. "But if you want to be artistic, you need to run, really hard and really far," he says, laughing. Will ran to Philadelphia, where he attended the University of the Arts and launched his career. Now thirty-four years old, with the playful enthusiasm of a teenager and the focus of a serious businessman, Will explains that changing his thinking has been a key to both getting in his lane and being the best he can be. "All of those tapes that spin in your head, it's real difficult to turn those off," he notes.

In chapter 1, Will described overcoming his rigid religious training and the stereotypes of black men that made him think he could not save and invest money. He says there have been many other times when changing his thoughts enabled a dramatic change in his circumstances. For example, he recalls his first day teaching music at a charter school in a difficult urban neighborhood when he was in his twenties. "I'm facing these children with my demon," he begins. "My demon is that as a child from a small town I was terrified of black people from underprivileged city neighborhoods. So I have all these tapes playing in my head: How am I going to do this? They're not going to respect me because I don't have the street *thang*—you know, I don't talk with the ghetto vernacular." Will was so scared of the students he spent the first ten minutes of class taking roll. Finally he said to himself, "You have something to give these kids. This is all in your mind."

Suddenly Will was able to mute the negative internal voices and just start teaching. He becomes emotional recalling how his expectations of the students changed after that first day: "Once I saw them as people, as so few teachers do, once I saw them as human beings just trying to grow and learn and navigate the world like every other kid, they didn't feel like they had to protect themselves anymore. That made them free to open their minds and take in what was given to them." He says the giving became mutual: "We fell in love with each other." Will wasn't like the men on the street that the kids respected but feared, he explains. "I was different from anybody that they had ever encountered, so there was a novelty factor that allowed me to get inside of their heads. They didn't have to be all reverent. They could just be themselves. So my trip wasn't even important because they had their own trip. We were able to empower each other to change."

A more recent empowering experience was watching the election of Barack Obama as president of the United States. "I get emotional even thinking about it now," he says, explaining that before Obama's election he assumed "anything but that" was possible for a black man in America. "I couldn't bring myself to believe it was possible," he explains, noting that he had accepted it as a thing that could not be changed. Throughout the campaign, Will was impressed with Obama's "brilliantly executed political strategy," but even more with the fact that Obama believed from the beginning that he could win. "Now I understand that we all limit ourselves. Every single person has that one thing they think is impossible," he observes, but an "extreme accomplishment" like Obama's can force people to think bigger. "I have really gigantic, insane goals that I was afraid to voice before, and I didn't even know I was afraid to voice them," he admits. "Watching the election news on CNN that night was a major growing experience." Will concludes that instead of trying to change other people, every single person needs to change his or her own thinking. That's how the world can change, he asserts.

CHANGE FROM WHAT TO WHAT?

Will's story illustrates several important points. Changing the way you think can have a tremendous effect on your experience, though, as he notes, changing your thoughts can be difficult. One thing that helped Will was acknowledging the kinds of social conditioning he discussed in chapter 1, so he could stop playing the tapes in his head that someone else had put there. By focusing on what he had to give the students, rather than on his fear of them, he was able to have a much greater impact as a teacher than if he had set out to change them. It helped that he was aware of his own thoughts. "I can't think of a time when I changed my mind before I was aware of what changing my mind meant," he adds.

When I talk about changing your mind, it is not to become someone different from who you really are. It is to strip away the socially conditioned, limiting thoughts of the False Self to discover the person you were made to be, focusing on your deep joy instead of your superficial wants or fears. Incidentally, this usually has a bigger impact on other people. Will wanted the students to respect him, but that desire came from his ego. The thought that really changed his attitude was, "You have something to give these kids." That was the voice of his inner wisdom, the voice that was aware of the greatest good. The transforming experience he had teaching came from thinking not about what he wanted for himself, but about what he was able to give his students. That focus brought him more respect than fighting for respect would have.

You may think of being true to yourself as something selfish, but when you are true to your deepest self you are actually more likely to be of service to others, as shown in many of the stories of transformation told in this book. By dealing with his own addiction, Matthew Cole has been able to help other alcoholics, including many teenagers. By quitting her corporate job and becoming a writer, Hilary Beard has moved from selling people unhealthy drinks to giving them information that can improve their health and well-being. By learning to deal with her own depression, Yvonne Thompson has been able to help other older people suffering from it, while Hollister Knowlton has moved into environmental work that will potentially have a bigger impact on the earth than the job where she felt stuck. When Hollister was stuck thinking, "Maybe I'm not capable of changing anything," that thought contributed to her depression, and it also prevented her from doing good in the world.

There has been much written lately about "the law of attraction," the idea that your thoughts determine what you manifest in your life. Although it is misleading to oversimplify this concept, it is certainly true that your expectations have a great influence on what you can and cannot accomplish, though in my experience, the law of attraction works best when you are focused on what you can give, rather than on what you can get out of a situation. When you are listening to your inner wisdom and thinking of the greatest good, you are more likely to have the experience of "way opening." Things fall into place more easily than when you are just focused on yourself. This may be because you are more in tune with "God's loving design," as Marcelle Martin put it. It may also be that you are less likely to waste energy anxiously worrying about the concerns of your own ego.

I learned the power of my thoughts when I was a canvasser for a grassroots organization. Every night I went out knocking on doors, asking people to write a check to support lobbying for health care reform or stronger environmental legislation.

Although the people I spoke to were free to choose their own responses, my attitude and expectations had a tremendous effect on whether those responses were positive or negative. When I was centered and feeling confident in my message, people opened their doors and their wallets to me. When I was negative or anxious about performing well, people picked up on it and closed their doors. I could literally measure my attitude in the dollars I raised. I soon learned that when I was off to a bad start, I should stop and take a break. Breathing deeply, laughing with another canvasser, putting the night in perspective, or remembering why I cared about the cause could all shift me into a more positive mind-set. My attitude change almost always translated into a greater reception from the people I was talking to. At national conferences I saw that the most successful canvassers in the country varied in age, size, race, and gender. What they had in common was an expectation of success.

Although my two and a half years as a canvasser convinced me of the power of our thoughts, becoming the director of a canvass operation also taught me that controlling our thoughts is much easier said than done. As I hired and trained people, I realized that some found believing in themselves to be quite easy—whether because of their innate personality or their social conditioning—while others found it extremely difficult. Sometimes people's self-doubts stemmed from deep issues that could not be swept away with a simple positive-thinking exercise, and telling them to "just think positively" was unhelpful, if not cruel. In particular, it was difficult to convince people that their attitude made a difference until they had the chance to see the difference themselves. Often a person who had a bad night would say, "This neighborhood is unfriendly," which only set them up for failure if we were returning to the same neighborhood the next night. Successful canvassers were the ones who recognized that one unfriendly person did not define a whole neighborhood. They also didn't take rejection personally.

In chapter 1, Martin Seligman, author of *Learned Optimism: How to Change Your Mind and Your Life*, argues that the way you explain negative events to yourself is often shaped by the way your parents explained negative events, and this pattern powerfully shapes how you respond to present-day challenges. In particular, if you assume a problem is permanent, pervasive, or personal (the three Ps), you are less likely to try to solve it. To overcome such negative thinking, he suggests that you monitor disempowering thoughts and argue with yourself, as Will did when he thought, "These kids are never going to respect me," and told himself in response, "You have something to give these kids. This is all in your mind." Seligman says it is particularly effective to list facts that disprove your negative assumptions, so he suggests you train yourself to look for evidence that refutes the three Ps. Finding such evidence was helpful to Hilary Beard when she was considering leaving her corporate career to pursue writing.

In addition to the mistrust of God and the family history she described in chapter 1, Hilary says her fear of economic insecurity was also rooted in her belief that a black woman could not support herself as a writer. Then Hilary discovered three books that shattered her preconception: Toni Morrison's *Beloved*, Alice Walker's *Possessing the Secret of Joy*, and Terry McMillan's *Waiting to Exhale*. Hilary gets out the hardcovers and demonstrates turning them over to reveal the beautiful photos of three black women. "I'm staring at three faces, and they look like me. So this belief that I have goes poof. It's like *The Wizard of Oz*. The curtain gets pulled back. This thing I believed is obviously not true anymore. So I started taking writing classes." Her new way of thinking enabled new action.

Hilary points out that her concerns about racism in the publishing industry were not unfounded; it was just that the industry had begun to change, and she was wise enough to recognize a new opportunity. Similarly, Barack Obama was able to see a change in American politics, even though many advisers told him that the United States was not ready to elect a black man. His optimism was not based on fantasy or wishful thinking. He had simply trained himself to look for evidence that supported his optimism, just as Seligman suggests. As Obama himself explained it in a *60 Minutes* interview, he knew he could win over white voters around the country because he had already done it in Illinois. In other words, although he recognized that racism still existed, he did not assume that it was permanent or pervasive, two of the three Ps that typify negative thinking.

In *Freeing Your Child from Negative Thinking*, child psychologist Tamar Chansky explains the third P, the assumption that problems are personal, or all about you. For example, a teacher isn't smiling one day, and a child thinks, "She's mad at me. She hates me," when in fact, the real reason is that the teacher's husband has just had surgery. Of course, adults are prone to the same kind of mistake—projecting an intention that might not be there—as we saw in the last chapter. To move past their erroneous assumptions to thoughts that are more accurate, Chansky suggests people ask themselves questions like, "What do I think is my part?" and "What parts may be about someone or something else?" She recommends that you be particularly alert for words like "never" and "always," for as she explains, "Negative thinking supersizes the problem; smart thinking is about 'specificizing' the problem." Often troubles shrink back to a realistic size when we relax, which, as Chansky points out, can reset our brains when they have gotten agitated. Instead of venting, which only increases the release of adrenaline, breathing deeply or taking a walk—the kinds of practices from chapter 2 that put us in touch with our True Selves—can help release us from negative thinking.

Tracey Smith-Diggs meditates and prays to calm her spirit, yet she still laughs about how things pop into her mind, including many judgments. To remind herself how she wants to live, she keeps a list of ancient Egyptian teachings on her bathroom wall. "The first one is 'Control your thoughts,' and that is really hard to do," she reiterates. " 'Control your actions' is number two," she notes. The ancient Egyptians were right to recognize the relationship between controlling your thoughts and controlling your actions. A student who expects to go to college is more likely to study than one who doesn't. A writer who believes she will be published is more likely to send her work to publishers. A musician who believes he does not have to be a starving artist is more likely to read the *Wall Street Journal* for financial advice. And a person who believes she will be elected is more likely to launch a campaign. Our thoughts are powerful, but part of the reason they are so powerful is that they often determine our actions.

Although our thoughts often precede our actions, sometimes we have to act, despite doubts and fears. We may have to be our own role models. We may have to show ourselves that we can change our circumstances before our minds really believe it. I noticed this when teaching people to canvass. There were skills that could help convey confidence to the people we spoke to, such as keeping eye contact and speaking concisely. Often learning the skills would help someone get their first few contributions so that real confidence followed. Likewise, when good canvassers lost their confidence, their eye contact would get shaky without them realizing it. Their thoughts and body language were interrelated, and changing their performance involved paying attention to both.

Because Buddhism puts a great emphasis on training our minds, I was surprised when practitioner Park Dong-Sun told me we should start by changing our actions. Born in Korea, where he studied the Korean form of Zen for decades, Dong-Sun is now in his late sixties and spends about two hours a day in walking meditation. With gray hair and searching brown eyes, he explains that if you strip Buddhism down to the basics, the message is this: "Do no evil or unwholesome deeds, and do many good deeds. Then when that is accomplished, try to purify your thoughts." He adds, "Most people can't get past stopping the evil."

For Dong-Sun, the behavior that was hard to stop was drinking alcohol. Although he had studied Buddhism intensely in Korea, he lost his way as an immigrant in the United States, experiencing a series of business failures, which accelerated his drinking. He remembers questioning, " 'What am I doing with my life? I am forty years old and I haven't accomplished many of my childhood ambitions and goals.' I was troubled. Then one day I went to the temple, and I met my teacher." After only half a day with the Zen master who later became head of the Buddhist order in Korea, Dong-Sun says, "Something happened to my psyche. I wanted to stop the way I was living." He found Alcoholics Anonymous, which he saw was helping people. "I wanted to be part of it and use their program to quit drinking, and that's what I did," he recalls. He had to translate some of the AA concepts from Judeo-Christian language into Zen Buddhist concepts, but the experience rekindled his desire to study and practice his own tradition.

Now sober for twenty-five years, Dong-Sun still attends meetings, though when new people come to AA talking about wanting to change, he sometimes asks them, "Change from what to what?" He explains that if you suffer from "stinking thinking"—as people in AA put it—then making a few changes in your life won't make much difference.

Dong-Sun is right. Millions of self-help books are sold every year to people hoping to change, but we have to ask ourselves, change in what way, for what purpose? Are we hoping to put on a new False Self, one that will make us more successful or popular? Or do we seek a deeper change, one that realigns our priorities and helps us to live more authentically? This is where listening within and knowing ourselves is crucial. It takes discernment to know what you should accept in yourself and what you should try to change.

Sometimes we are able to change our own thinking. Other times we have a sense of being given a new perspective, like Dong-Sun when he met his teacher or the people in chapter 3 who experienced reassurance that seemed to come unbidden from a greater source. This brings us back to the original Serenity Prayer quoted in the introduction. Unlike the more common version, Reinhold Niebuhr's prayer begins, "God, grant us grace," recognizing that sometimes we need help to accept the things we cannot change and to change those we should change. By asking for grace first, Niebuhr reminds us that we don't struggle alone. God has the power to change us, even when we are not able to change ourselves. The Hebrew Scriptures have some potent metaphors for this. In Malachi, God is compared to a refiner and purifier of silver. In Isaiah, God is the potter, and we are the clay. In both these craft metaphors, things get rather uncomfortable for the material being transformed; it is shaped and fired before it becomes truly useful. Many people have found these images to be meaningful reflections of their own experiences of spiritual formation.

In chapter 3, Ro'Bin White Morton described hearing God say, "Stand still and know that I am God," as she was rushing around the house. That incident was a turning point in her life, helping her to let go of her anxiety and preparing her to face her biggest challenge, Hurricane Katrina. The water was up to Ro'Bin's neck when she and her husband finally abandoned their New Orleans home, realizing that the water was not subsiding as it had during previous floods. "After we left, people died," she says. Ro'Bin and her husband made their way to the crowded Superdome, where they had to wait three long days for help. Ro'Bin sang hopeful songs to herself the whole time to keep up her spirits. In retrospect, she says that experience taught her how to sit and wait, something she has always found difficult. "I used to pray for patience," she recalls, joking that she hadn't really wanted the experience that finally taught her patience.

Not every experience of God changing us is dramatic or painful. My first memory of feeling a spiritual shift came during the summer before my senior year in high school. In addition to applying to college, in the coming year I would be president of the outing club; a member of the chorus, math team, hockey team, and lacrosse team; and most intimidating, editor of the yearbook. The fact that two previous yearbook editors had melted under the pressure was weighing on me as much as the prospective work. Then one day as I was walking to the library a sudden sense of reassurance came to me. I don't remember a voice, just a deep sense that I would be all right. At the time I didn't think of it as God, but the sense stayed with me through the late nights and deadlines of the following year. Letting go of my anxiety made the workload manageable, and seeing things work out helped me learn to trust life.

Even when we don't have a dramatic spiritual experience that changes our thinking, cultivating an attitude of trust, rather than anxiousness, can make a huge difference in what we experience. Trusting doesn't mean that nothing challenging will ever happen. Serenity, after all, is a state of mind. It does not imply that the house is perfectly clean, the children perfectly behaved, the evening news all good. Serenity simply means that we are not agitated by the things that could be better. Although it might be nice if God calmed us down every time we needed it, there are also things we can do to help ourselves let go of anxiety.

LIVING WITH LOVE, NOT FEAR

Before becoming a parent, I never thought of myself as a fearful person. I had been skydiving and rock climbing. I had hitchhiked in the Middle East and Africa. I didn't spend a lot of time thinking about danger. As soon as I had a baby, however, I started noticing all the potential baby killers in my home: buttons, pennies, drapery cords, balloons—and that's not even counting the chemicals under the sink. One day I found my six-month-old daughter sucking on a piece of broken glass, a thin line of blood running off her smiling lip. I felt the absolute terror of realizing I was not totally in control.

After twelve years of parenthood, I've now survived enough trips to the emergency room with bloody children to accept that we never know when a foot is going to slip or a bike hit a bump. For that matter, we don't know when a plane is going to crash into a building or when the only vegetable our kid eats will be hit with E. coli. We never know, and loving a vulnerable child can make this not-knowing nerve-racking.

Of course there are things we can do to decrease the risks. We can plug up the electric sockets (until our children learn to take the plastic plug-fillers out); we can tie up the drapery cords (until they learn to climb on the windowsill); we can lock the medicine cabinet (until they learn the combination), but we can't insure against everything. I know of a three-year-old who tragically hung himself on a bush with the strap of his bike helmet. How could a parent possibly foresee such a horrible use of something they bought to keep their child safe?

I believe in bike helmets and car seats and safety locks on the medicine cabinets. We all have a responsibility to look out for the safety of ourselves and others, especially children. But our culture has gotten so safety-obsessed that we've lost the "Trust in God" half of Mohammed's teaching: "Trust in God, and tie up your camels." There's something profoundly realistic in the Arabic phrase *Insha'Allah*, which means "If God wills it," said by Muslims whenever they make a plan. Malik Mubashshir, who studied comparative religion at Harvard, points out that this idea is in the Judeo-Christian scriptures, too. Paraphrasing the Epistle of James, he says, "Don't say tomorrow I will do such and such. Say, 'If God wills, tomorrow I will do such and such.' The book of Proverbs says, 'Boast not yourself of tomorrow, for thou knowest not what a day will bring forth.' There is that sense all throughout the Semitic traditions. You don't know the future. Your plans exist within a larger plan."

The realization that we do not control the future can be frightening, but it can also bring us peace if we are able to trust the larger plan. With a brown head scarf fastened beneath her chin, Fatima bin Mustafa admits that living with trust can be a struggle. "I'm just sort of a controlling type of person," she says. "I need to know everything that is going to be. I'm not a risk taker. I do a lot of research before I make a decision. I observe a lot." Fatima also confesses to being paranoid about germs. Three weeks ago her son said, "Mom, why do you wash your hands so much? You're just living in fear." Fatima notes, "That was from Allah to me. Sometimes Allah uses people to speak to you. So I had to realize, whatever Allah wants for me is going to happen. I said, 'You know what, sweetie, you're absolutely right. We can just do the best that we can do.' " Fatima says she has been consciously trying not to be so fearful.

So how do you let go of fear and cultivate trust? Trust does not always come in a dramatic spiritual insight. Sometimes it grows gradually, as we nervously take each step. Marcelle Martin used to be afraid that God would ask her to do more than she was able, though as she has lived into her calling—teaching at Pendle Hill and publishing her writing—that fear has diminished. She still has little anxieties about things like being prepared for class, but she notes that it helps to focus on each task before her. "It's like one step at a time, and I'll focus on this step right now and try to do a good job with that, and the next step will follow," she explains. Sometimes she worries about an exercise in class flopping or other people judging her. "It's all about me, focusing on me instead of trusting the Spirit and trusting that there are other people in the room through whom things can come, and it's not all about my planning or preparation. Some of it is the habit of anxiety," she notes. "It's related to fundamentally not trusting ourselves, fundamentally not trusting life, trying to be in control, trying to protect ourselves from fear, painful emotion, and embarrassment. The anxiety is related to that need to control instead of just accepting ourselves and the situation, life as it is."

Letting go of our anxiety and need to control is one way to deal with fear. As Marcelle indicates, we need to accept ourselves and life as it is, even as we do what we can to be prepared. But sometimes our fear comes from the knowledge that there is something we should change, something we should not just accept passively. In such cases we need courage as well as serenity. It may be the courage to risk what is familiar or to risk upsetting those close to us. In extreme cases it may be the courage to risk our personal safety. In any case, fear can be paralyzing if we do not get past it. Courage does not mean the absence of fear, just the ability to overcome it.

Taking little steps is one way to get past fear, something Hilary Beard practiced when she began pursuing her dream of becoming a writer. "In corporate America when you want to accomplish something big, you break it down—chunk, chunk, chunk—but you do something every day, so by the end of the year, boom, the thing is done." Hilary applied her corporate training to her new goal, breaking it down into tiny tasks that were not too scary. "So literally what was not too scary to do was to take the phone book to work one day. That was not too scary," she recalls. "Then the next day what was not too scary was to look up all the colleges in the area that might have an adult education program and write down their phone numbers. Then the next day it was not too scary to call them and see if they had a catalog." She retraces the steps: reading the catalogs, picking a course, registering for a writing class. "Going to the course, that was scary, but by then I was excited," she adds with a smile.

There is much wisdom in Hilary's method. Often we make change seem overwhelming by focusing on the large goal when focusing on a small step would be more manageable and would build our trust for the next step. Taking small steps undermines fear and builds courage. It also helps to acknowledge our fears, rather than deny them. Only by admitting to ourselves what we fear can we work through that feeling. The trick is to acknowledge fear without getting stuck in it.

Although Tracey Smith-Diggs lives in a quiet, affluent neighborhood with tree-lined streets, the schools where she leads pregnancy-prevention programs are surrounded by poverty and violence. Tracey has made a conscious choice not to tap into the fear of the people around her, explaining that she wouldn't be able to do her work if she did. "One of the things I have control over is, I don't watch the news," says Tracey. "What I see and deal with every day is enough. That's all I can handle." Her mother worries that Tracey is working in the "O.K. Corral," but Tracey tries to focus on her faith. "I'm just going to base my life on trusting the Holy Spirit, no matter what I come up against," she says. This includes trust that the Holy Spirit will guide her when she needs to take precautions. "I've learned when a person or a situation doesn't feel right, I remove myself. I know it, and I'm out of there. I'm always trying to be sensitive."

Although she does not believe in being reckless, Tracey notes that many people get caught in an exaggerated sense of fear, including her mother and her husband. "I don't want bars on the windows. If it was up to me I wouldn't even have any curtains up there, but this is the best I can do," she says, laughing at the sheer curtains that were a compromise with her husband. "I've just learned not to let other people's fear come on me. People may steal all the wood in our backyard," she says, pointing to a large pile of firewood they chopped from a fallen tree. "I can't live in that fear day to day. So that's something I'm trying to let go of with the Holy Spirit, praying that I won't be fearful, because then I wouldn't be able to go in and do what I do, and who else is going to do it?"

It is all too easy to fear other people, whether because they are on the other side of town, the other side of a political conflict, or the other side of the world. Dividing people into "us" and "them" is one of those common patterns of thought that is especially difficult to break. In fact, it may take a dramatic experience to enable us to see the humanity in those we have been taught to fear or hate. Father Michael Doyle describes the experience that changed the way he thinks about such divisions and the violence that often accompanies them.

Michael had grown up in rural Ireland, where he heard heroic stories of the old men who, as part of the original Irish Republican Army, had fought for Ireland's independence from Britain in the early twentieth century. One day during the 1950s, when Michael was a teenager, he helped his cousin deliver a cow to one such local hero, Seamus McKeon, whose farm was in the next parish. The two lads were invited in for tea by the fire, and Seamus, who was about seventy by then, began talking about his youth, recalling a day during the war when he and two other men were hiding in a safe house. When they were warned that two British soldiers were approaching, Seamus opened the window and shot one dead. A comrade shot the other. The IRA men took everything off the corpses and ran across fields and hedges for three hours to get as far away as possible. That night, when they finally looked at what they had taken, they found a letter from the mother of the soldier Seamus had shot, telling her son, "Now, you're in a war, but always be good to the people."

Father Michael had grown up hearing his grandfather tell the story of the horse and cart that had been wheeled into town with the dead bodies of "two Tans," short for "Black and Tans," a nickname for the British. Before hearing Seamus's account of the killing, they had been "two Tans," not real men with mothers.

"It was beautiful what the mother said," recalls Father Michael. "And Seamus McKeon sitting there by the fire smoking his pipe fifty years later, said, 'He was twenty-two, and I was twenty-two. We could have gone into Arvagh and had a pint of Guinness. And he was dead in the lane.' It was a lament," Father Michael observes, explaining that the story made him realize how people were dehumanized by war. "It pulled the glamour out of the whole thing for me," he explains. "That changed me."

Hearing the old man's lament—which humanized the people Father Michael had grown up thinking of as the enemy—had a profound impact on the direction of his life. Now the pastor of Sacred Heart Church, Father Michael is aware that many of his middle-class parishioners who drive to church from the suburbs fear the poor people who live in the parish neighborhood. Sacred Heart tries to tackle that fear by giving people of different backgrounds the opportunity to celebrate and work together. Pointing to the record of Jesus's life, he observes, "The one plea that is more prevalent than any other is 'Do not be afraid.' Fear is the crippling emotion," he explains. "Fear has prevented more good from being done than any other reality."

Recognizing the good she is doing helps Tracey Smith-Diggs overcome fear. She thinks of what she can give the students who don't have many other positive role models, an approach that can be applied in a variety of situations. Thinking about the needs of others can take you out of your own obsessive worries. It shifts your perspective, making whatever you fear seem less important. As the Dalai Lama writes in *The Compassionate Life*: "If you have a sense of caring for others, you will manifest a kind of inner strength in spite of your own difficulties and problems."

Through compassion and caring for others, he adds, "you gain inner strength, self-confidence, courage, and a greater sense of calm. This is a clear example of how one's way of thinking can really make a difference."

Although you can often change your experience by changing your thinking, there are many things you just cannot control alone. For Celeste Zappala, the most painful has been the war in Iraq, which took her thirty-year-old son Sherwood in 2004. "I knew going into it that the war was wrong, and I wasn't powerful enough to change it," explains Celeste from behind her large desk where she heads a social service agency. As a woman who has advocated for others for decades, Celeste says losing Sherwood has meant coming to terms with the limits of her own power, though she notes she still has the power to decide how she's going to respond to her loss. "It's horrible, and it's unfair, but what do you do? You can do nothing and just be really angry, or you can try to act from a place of compassion," she explains.

For Celeste, acting out of love and compassion, rather than hate and bitterness, is essential. She says that after Sherwood was blown off his Humvee, her family agreed to speak out against the war to make sure his death would not be co-opted by people who wanted to promote a glorious image of the conflict. "But I also realized that we needed to say these things with a loving heart, and not with great bitterness and anger," she explains, citing Martin Luther King, Jr. as her model. "It's hard not to hate the people, not only who were responsible for Sherwood's death directly, but those who sent him there, who take no responsibility for it, who don't want anybody to think about it, and who continued to send more and more people there without plan, support, or reason," says Celeste with a note of frustration in her voice. "That would be an easy spot to take, and I could do it," she says firmly. With her voice quiet and calm again she continues, "But the harder spot is to say, 'This is not what God asks of us. God asks us to love, even the people who we have great animosity toward in our hearts.' " She cites King's famous line, "I have decided to stick with love. Hate is too great a burden to bear."

Celeste hasn't completely overcome her anger. "I'm not Martin Luther King. I'm not Jesus. I can't overcome it. I just try to turn away from it." She says with a laugh that when she can't love people, she tries to at least not hate them. "When you put that mantle of hatred on, you armor yourself with all that stuff—you can't move. You become what you're fighting against." Celeste also believes she will be more effective if she speaks to people with respect. Although she can't convince everyone, she says, "I can talk to people who will listen to me." In fact many people are listening as Celeste now speaks all over the United States, as well as internationally. Her hope is that they will commit themselves to building a more just and peaceful world. She notes that many important social changes were slow, uphill battles, like ending slavery and winning women's suffrage. "But that doesn't give us the option to be off the hook," says Celeste. "We still choose the path we're on." She says it is very meaningful to her when people say that her words have touched their hearts and moved them to a deeper commitment.

When I hear stories like Celeste's, of people choosing love over anger, even when they have lost a child to violence, it puts my own petty angers in perspective. To think I got angry when my children wrote on the beige carpet with pink sidewalk chalk.

To think I stomped out of the room when my mother asked if I was pregnant when I was really just a few pounds overweight. Sometimes thinking of people like Celeste is enough to dissolve our irritations, but sometimes seeing our angers as petty just makes us feel guilty about them. In such cases, denying our feelings is not likely to help.

"When you are angry with someone, please don't pretend that you are not angry," writes the Buddhist monk and teacher Thich Nhat Hanh in his book *Anger*. Instead he suggests being tender with yourself so that you can see and take care of the situation that is causing your suffering. He compares compassion to the equipment that firefighters use to put out a fire and suggests that you recognize that the person you are angry with is probably suffering, too. By speaking to that person honestly and with compassion, you can transform situations that seem hopeless. Even if the other person will not engage in dialogue, you can change your own experience by being mindful, breathing deeply, and accepting the situation. A Vietnamese monk who lived through war in his own country, Hanh believes this approach is a key to personal, familial, and world peace.

Although there are differences in the ways religions talk about anger, compassion and forgiveness are themes in all the world's spiritual traditions. "There is this very ferocious image of Muslims," notes Malik Mubashshir. "If somebody does us a wrong, we're supposed to retaliate immediately. It's funny because the principle of an 'eye for an eye' is recognized as a principle of justice. It's in the Torah. It's in the Talmud. But it's side by side in Islam with a Jesus-like ethic that says it is better to turn the other cheek. It is better to forgive someone who did something wrong.

Yes, you have a right to justice if you're the injured party, but if you can forgive it is better." He explains that if people are only told to forgive, they will feel guilty when they can't and will slip into a victimized mentality. Islam, he says, teaches, "Yeah, you were wronged. You have a right to be angry and to expect some compensation, but are you capable of rising to something higher than that? One of my favorite things about Islam is my sense that it has balance."

As Imam Malik suggests, the ideal of forgiveness can compound a person's suffering if it just makes them feel bad about themselves. This is especially true of women, who are often socialized not to admit their anger. The trick is to acknowledge anger, without getting stuck in blame, which is disempowering, rather than empowering. Only when you have acknowledged your anger can you discern whether it is a sign that you need to change something or accept what cannot be changed.

Sally Jergesen was both angry and hurt when her husband walked out on her and their young son. She felt betrayed again when, the day after signing a mediated settlement, she found out he would be making much more money in his new job than she had believed when she decided not to ask for alimony. Then, only months after their separation, he moved in with his new girlfriend and, without telling Sally, began bringing their son there for overnights, breaking their mediation agreement. "I was so angry I couldn't fall asleep until three in the morning," she recalls.

Although Sally has found some self-help books to be helpful in learning to let go of her anger, she complains about the books that suggest that you only need to think positively and positive things will happen. "It makes it seem like it's all in your control, and that's not always empowering," she says, explaining that when she has a negative thought, she thinks, "Oh, I'm having a negative thought! Bad things are going to happen. Clearly I'm screwing myself!" Like Marcelle Martin, she has come to realize that she needs to let herself feel her difficult emotions, rather than bury them. On the other hand, she notes, "I've come to a place where it's time for me to stop living in those sad and angry emotions and start doing things for myself. It's somewhat of an organic process. I've tried not to force myself to do things before I'm ready."

The distinction Sally makes between feeling her emotions and living in them is important. If you believe you shouldn't feel anger, you might deny your feelings, pushing them under a mask of contentment that isn't real. This will only make listening to your deepest wisdom more difficult. On the other hand, accepting your difficult emotions need not mean getting stuck in them, wearing them like armor, as Celeste Zappala put it. Carrying anger for many years can weigh you down, hurting you more than the object of your anger.

Changing Your Habits

It is probably not that helpful to tell a really angry person that they are learning something valuable, but it is good to tell yourself. If this doesn't work, look back on past experiences that made you angry and see if you can appreciate them from a different perspective now. Rabbi Zalman Schachter-Shalomi recommends this in *From Age-ing to Sage-ing*, a book that explores how people can harvest their life experiences and turn them into wisdom. He recalls his own painful experience of getting fired from his first congregation by someone whom he had spent a good deal of time helping. "For years my mind flashed red with anger whenever I thought about this act of human injustice," recalls Schachter-Shalomi. Eventually, however, he realized that many better opportunities had come to him as a result, giving him much more influence than he would have had if he had stayed in that congregation. "If my so-called malefactor had not fired me, I would probably still be in my first pulpit," he notes. In a workshop, I once heard Schachter-Shalomi share that he has a thanksgiving party in his mind every year. He imagines all the people whom he could hold a grudge against and thanks them for whatever gift their actions brought. This practice helps him to feel at peace.

Gratitude is a habit recommended by every spiritual tradition, as well as by contemporary science. Recent research has confirmed what humans have known for centuries—that counting your blessings really does change your perspective. It's not just that we should feel grateful; feeling grateful changes us. One study showed representative results. When participants were asked to find something to appreciate every day, they:

- Felt better about their lives.
- Were more optimistic.
- Were more energetic.
- Were more enthusiastic.
- Were more determined.

- Were more joyful.
- Exercised more.
- Had fewer illnesses.
- Got more sleep.
- Were more likely to have helped someone else.

These results show that finding something to appreciate may be one of the most effective ways to change your outlook. It is much easier than overcoming difficult feelings like fear or anger, though focusing on blessings can diminish those feelings, as well. It is also a habit that need not be time-consuming. In our home at bedtime we gather around and list things we are grateful for: a sunny afternoon, a playdate. For me, the chance to write is a common gratitude. My son often says, "French fries," which is fine. He is appreciating the little things, even if I wish he'd say broccoli.

GRATITUDE PRAYER

There is no simpler prayer than to say, "Thank you, God, for . . ." and list the things you appreciate in your life. Following this practice regularly can magnify your feelings of contentment and shrink your irritations. Some days the list will be long and include special events like the birth of a niece or a visit from an old friend. Other days you might feel hard-pressed to come up with anything special, but there are always blessings to be counted. Something as ordinary as "Thank you for the food we eat" can remind you that billions of people in the world cannot afford adequate food. Remembering them is not intended to make you feel guilty about your dinner, but to make you aware of something you may take for granted.

Often it is the greatest blessings in our lives that we take for granted, like our health or our families. I find it particularly helpful to thank God for my children when I am feeling annoyed by them, which sometimes happens when they are poking each other during prayer time. I will suddenly remember what blessings my children are, even in their exasperating moments, which are, after all, helping to teach me patience. Being able to see the gifts in such challenges and truly appreciate them isn't always easy, but through practice, it is a habit that can help to cultivate serenity.

When my children were younger and I was sleep-deprived and cranky, I started a gratitude journal. I followed Oprah Winfrey's suggestion to write three things every day, even if one of them was "still breathing." It really did help to remember that my energetic children were healthy and my husband supportive, even if I sometimes felt abandoned when he went to work eight hours a day. (The fact that he had a job to go to was a blessing I often overlooked.) There were moments when I needed a jolt to realize how much I regularly took for granted. I remember a dinner party where tables were arranged on a stately wraparound porch. I had just sat down with a plate of delicious-looking food when I saw my then-two-year-old son throwing the driveway gravel at the hosts' car. I leaped from my seat and hauled him back onto the porch with a loud sigh. The woman I was sitting next to—an old friend who remembered that my son had had some health scares during his first year of life—said, "Well, he sure looks healthy now."

"Yeah," I said sarcastically. "Aren't I lucky that I have a son healthy enough to throw rocks at cars?" It wasn't until the next morning as I sat in silence during Quaker meeting for worship that it hit me how profoundly lucky I was.

For me, sitting in silent worship for an hour every Sunday has been a bedrock habit. Even when having babies interrupted my daily meditation practice, there was always child care at meeting to give me an hour to center. The fact that there are other people there, and a set time period, helps to keep me in my seat, rather than jumping up to put the laundry in the dryer, as I am tempted to do when I meditate at home. Sometimes an insight will come to me in the silence, like my realization that I was indeed lucky to have a child healthy enough to throw rocks at cars. Sometimes another person will receive an insight, and they will stand and share it with the community. Other times nothing dramatic happens, just a subtle lightening of whatever I am carrying or a chance to remember who I am outside of social roles. Of course, Quaker meeting is not the only way to have these experiences, though I would argue that everyone needs some silence in their lives, even if it's just leaving the iPod at home when you're walking the dog or turning off the car radio once in a while. That space not only lets us hear our own thoughts, it makes room for us to hear the Divine. The reassurance I felt walking to the library as a nervous high school student might not have come if I had been wearing headphones.

Many of the practices we discussed in chapter 2 that help us to know ourselves can also help us to change our mental habits: meditation, centering prayer, and self-inventories, for example. If you do not have such a practice yourself, Park Dong-Sun advises you to start with five minutes of meditation a day. Although he explains that there are many levels of meditation, he says one of the most basic is to seek serenity by concentrating on one meditative object at a time. "Sometimes people spend their whole lifetime on that level," he notes. "What it does is calm the mind and improve concentration." He says this helps you to see more than just the surface level of things, even appreciating the "ultimate mystery" of things at their molecular level. Studies show that this sort of regular practice really does change you. Not only does meditation decrease anxiety and blood pressure, but new scientific evidence shows that it actually changes your mental wiring. One monk who had spent years meditating on compassion participated in a study where he was put in an MRI and shown images meant to stimulate compassion. Interestingly, the images triggered a different part of his brain than they did in most people. Instead of getting sad or hopeless—suffering from what some people call "compassion fatigue"—the needs of others triggered his love.

In Sharon Begley's *Train Your Mind, Change Your Brain: How a New Science Reveals Our Extraordinary Potential to Transform Ourselves*, the Dalai Lama writes, "Buddhist practitioners familiar with the workings of the mind have long been aware that it can be transformed through training. What is exciting and new is that scientists have now shown that such mental training can also change the *brain*. Related to this is evidence that the brain adapts or expands in response to repeated patterns of activity, so that in a real sense the brain we develop reflects the life we lead. This has far-reaching implications for the effects of habitual behavior in our lives, especially the positive potential of discipline and spiritual practice."

Disciplined spiritual practice can be one of the benefits of being part of an organized religion or a community like AA. For those who have rebelled against the rigidity or sexism of a traditional religion, it can be tempting to adopt the comforting or fashionable aspects of various traditions, while avoiding the hard parts. You may wear Buddhist beads, attend a Native American sweat lodge, visit a friend for Passover, or go to church on Christmas, but never participate in a community that challenges your False Self. In fact most religious traditions have practices that are difficult, like tithing or fasting, which are meant to strip away your selfish parts and develop qualities like gratitude and compassion. By practicing one tradition deeply you can benefit from such challenges, which can also help to transform your attitude.

Fatima bin Mustafa tells me about her experience fasting during the Muslim month of Ramadan, which ended a month before our interview. "This was the most physically difficult Ramadan I've ever had," says Fatima, who was still regaining her strength after a bout of pneumonia. Getting up to eat before the sunrise prayer at five-fifteen and then fasting until sunset was also more difficult because the days were long, which will be true for the next several years as Ramadan moves through the summer on a lunar cycle. In addition to fasting, she prayed many times during the day, read the Qur'an, and continued her usual responsibilities—working and caring for her two children, who only fasted in the morning. She recalls her third-grader looking at the clock and asking her mother the time every fifteen minutes. Fatima said to her, "Can you imagine not looking forward to a time to eat because you have nothing to eat for days and days and days?" She notes that fasting can help to develop gratitude, as well as compassion for those who have less, though she still often felt cranky near the end of the day when she was hungry and exhausted. "It's a very intense period," she explains. "If you don't grow spiritually from that, you have to reevaluate what you're doing because you should feel different. You should think differently. You should have a peace about you, a patience." In the end, Fatima says this Ramadan was "glorious" because the greater difficulty made it more rewarding.

The idea of voluntarily doing without something is profoundly countercultural these days, but sometimes giving something up makes room for something better. In chapter 2, Hollister Knowlton shared how giving up her car, her job, and eating animal products helped her engage a joyful commitment to environmental work. Giving up little habits like subscribing to magazines helped to prepare Hal Taussig to be more generous with his money once he started making a lot of it. Tracey Smith-Diggs mentioned giving up listening to the news as something that helps her control fear.

Habits like watching television can affect us in ways we do not even realize. Becca Levy, a social psychologist at Yale University's School of Medicine, studied the negative stereotypes of older people on television and how they affect older viewers. She found that the more television older people watched, the more likely they were to think of their own age group as helpless, sick, grumpy, or senile, like many sitcom characters. In another study she found that those exposed to such stereotypes of aging "tend to get more forgetful, walk more slowly, and have higher blood pressure and lower will to live" than those who were told that aging leads to wisdom. Television affected their thoughts, and their thoughts affected their behavior. Obviously an easy way to change this cycle would be to watch less television and/or limit oneself to shows that do not show negative stereotypes.

There are many negative messages in our culture, and although it may be impossible to avoid them altogether, we can consciously choose what we want to feed our minds. Although I haven't given up the news habit completely, I do try to avoid programs that get their ratings by fueling fear. It is important to know that some toys contain lead, and some foods E. coli, but if we let ourselves get hooked by all the "Special Report at Eleven" ads, we'll walk around afraid of everything in our closets and refrigerators, not to mention our neighbors. At a certain point we have to reject the culture of fear, recognizing that social conditioning is not just something that happens to us when we are young; it happens continually. Likewise, I try to limit my exposure to magazines or ads that portray all women as skinny teenagers, knowing they don't do much for my love of my own body. I try not to focus on anything that is deliberately trying to mess with my serenity.

The same can be said of people, though they can be harder to turn the page on. Will Brock mentioned that his small hometown was a great place to learn basic values, but it was not supportive of his creativity, so he had to move to a bigger city. When Hilary Beard first started writing, she enjoyed hanging out with artists and poets because she found it fostered her creativity, but as she became more serious about pursuing writing professionally, she noticed that many of these creative people recounted starving-artist stories over and over again, perpetuating her fear that she wouldn't be able to make money as a writer. Realizing that their thoughts affected her own, she stopped hanging out with people who didn't believe it was possible to make a living from their creativity.

It is good to be aware of our social habits and make conscious choices about who we want to spend time with. Sometimes our social habits need to change as we move into different stages of growth. Park Dong-Sun advises people new to AA, "If you want to keep this newly found spiritual way of life, don't be away from the community too long or you will return to your old way of life very easily. Sometimes family and friends will force you to come back to your old way of life to justify their living." There is much evidence that other people do affect both our attitudes and our actions. For example, studies show that married people are five to six times more likely to make healthy changes in their lives, like quitting smoking or drinking, if their spouses do, too. That is why we can't just talk about changing ourselves in isolation. We are social beings. Other people affect us, and we affect them. In fact, learning when to just accept other people, and when to try to influence them, is often one of the most painful and personal challenges of the wisdom to know the difference.

Queries

What thoughts do you regularly have that you would like to change?

How did you learn these patterns of thinking?

Have you ever experienced a dramatic shift in perspective?

Can you tell the difference between a dramatic shift and an attempt to bury your feelings?

What do you most often fear?

What most often angers you?

When do you feel compassion?

What triggers your gratitude?

Do you have any current practices that help you keep a positive attitude?

Are there new practices you would like to adopt?

Five

PRACTICING LOVING ACCEPTANCE

As a lifelong educator, Joan Countryman has made a career of trying to influence others in positive ways, though she acknowledges it is not something she can control or measure. "It is an interesting challenge for teachers to believe that they're making a difference because sometimes you don't even have a glimmer of it," laughs Joan, who is best known for her work as interim director of the Oprah Winfrey Leadership Academy for Girls in South Africa. She suspects that teachers have more influence than they realize, but compares teaching to opening a door for someone and then getting out of the way. Joan gives the example of teaching math, which she did for twenty-three years before becoming a school principal. "I loved teaching math," she says. "It is a discipline where you spend a lot of time trying to convince students that they can understand it and do something with it." It is hard to know how building confidence and motivation will influence a student's life, but Joan says, "Education has a spiritual dimension." A Quaker herself, Joan explains that the Quaker school where she taught for many years looked for "that of God in every person." She adds, "What I think teaching is about is finding that spark of Truth in each person."

Joan's optimism that what she does matters came from her parents and from the era when she was growing up. "There was Rosa Parks. There was *Brown Versus Board of Education*. There were the Little Rock Nine," she recalls. These events were central to the dinner conversation in Joan's black family. "There was this sense that I could make a difference, that we could make a difference." She recalls learning the Serenity Prayer in high school and feeling that it was an affirmation of her ability to change things, though it also reminded her to choose where to put her energy. "On the one hand, I got this sense from my family that I could do whatever I wanted in the world," she recalls. "On the other hand, there were booby traps, hurdles that you had to negotiate." During segregation Joan's parents refused to travel in the Deep South, where they were born. When their family visited Baltimore or Washington, D.C., they packed their own lunch to avoid the indignity of segregated lunch rooms. Joan notes that her parents always insisted on being treated with respect despite the prejudice that was common in their era, something that influenced Joan.

Dressed in a colorful cotton skirt, Joan's self-confidence comes through in her posture, direct gaze, and easy laugh. It is easy to imagine her impressing Oprah and commanding the respect of a few hundred students, as she did as head of a prestigious girls' school for twelve years before she went to work in

South Africa. When I ask whether she thinks the way she carries herself influences how she is treated, she responds firmly, "All the time. It really makes a difference." She says it is hard to define, "but I know something that my parents gave me allows me to carry myself in the world expecting people to treat me in a humane and thoughtful way. Mostly they do, and I think that's why. That's something I'd love to teach kids," she adds, noting that her son-in-law teaches his children to always offer a firm handshake. "You can present yourself in ways that command respect," she concludes.

Joan's confidence shapes her actions as well as her attitude. On the day I interviewed her, she was preparing to visit South Africa with her husband, children, and grandchildren, but two of their passports had not yet arrived. Although many Americans were canceling travel plans because of widespread passport problems, Joan was not worried. "It was very clear to me that we were not just going to sit back and let them screw around and not give us our passports. We were going to get somebody to do something for us," she explains. Her son called his congressional representative in Michigan, while Joan called her senator in Rhode Island. "I'm confident this is all going to get straightened out," she says, joking that they had both houses of Congress working on their problem. "That is what they are for," she explains sincerely. "We live in a time now when a lot of people don't think that way." She says that one of the wonderful things about working in South Africa was seeing the hope students had in their ability to shape their young country.

Although Joan conveys confidence in her ability to impact her surroundings, she also seems at ease letting go of the things she cannot control. She gives the example of her children. "I've always thought that what you are supposed to do as a parent is to give your child an opportunity and just get out of the way," she says. "You don't really know if it is going to take or not. There are lots of examples along the way where you wish for something—like you wish they'd really love piano lessons," she says with a laugh. "What I tried to do with my own kids was think ahead to the fact that I was preparing them to leave home, and that they really were their lives, not mine."

It takes wisdom to know when to let children go and how far. Joan recalls that her young son often wanted to walk to the neighborhood store alone to buy the newspaper because he was learning to read by studying the names of baseball teams on the sports page. "I would say, 'You're not old enough to do that.' Then one day, I don't remember how old he was, but we were standing on the porch and he said, 'I'm going to get the paper.' And there was something about the way he said it that let me know that in fact he was ready. Obviously I was with him enough that I had a sense. It was more than those words, but there does come a moment when you know they are ready." She compares parenting to other forms of teaching: "It's a sense of trying to open the door for someone else," she reiterates.

How Your Attitude Impacts Others

Our dealings with other people are an important practice ground for the wisdom to know the difference. On the one hand, we have to accept that we cannot change anyone else. On the other hand, we need to realize that our behavior can influence others, and our behavior is in our control. Joan Countryman embodies this balance, illustrating how the lessons from the last chapter can be applied to our dealings with other people. When facing the passport delay, Joan did not assume the problem was permanent, pervasive, or personal, so she didn't waste energy worrying about it. Instead, she called her senator and asked for help. In general, she is willing to do what she can to make an impact because she is not paralyzed by fear. This centeredness enables her to ask for what she wants, while accepting the autonomy of others. For example, she accepts that she can't force her children to like piano or her students to like math, which ironically makes her a more effective parent and teacher. Although she is not naïve about the injustices people sometimes commit, she still seeks "that of God" in everyone. As we shall see, seeking the best in others makes us much more likely to find it. In fact, this is one of the areas where the "law of attraction" really works.

The stories in the last chapter hinted at the fact that changing the tapes in your head can affect how others respond to you. For instance, when Will Brock let go of his fear of his students, they became open to learning from him. Likewise, when I let go of my anxiety while canvassing, the people I approached became more open to my message, just as people became more open to Celeste Zappala's antiwar message when she was sticking with love. All of us felt most effective when we were focused on the greatest good, rather than our fear or egos. Other themes of this book, like knowing and accepting who you are, can also have a profound effect on your relationships with other people. Timothy Olsen recalls how coming out as a gay man helped him to see the good in his father: "I know he didn't change for the better because of my coming out, but my approach and acceptance of him changed. I accept him as he is with his faults, flaws, and foibles, and out of that ground of honesty we can be open with each other. We can have a good relationship, which we really couldn't have before with this cloud of fear hanging over me." Timothy notes that the same has been true in other relationships, as well. Many other people I interviewed also mentioned a connection between accepting themselves and accepting other people, which in turn affected how other people treated them.

If we look for "that of God in every person," as Quakers put it—treating people with compassion, rather than judgment—it can change the dynamic between us. Seeing what Rabbi Erin Hirsh called "sparks of the Divine" can happen more often than we expect, if we are looking for them. Rabbi Erin used to work in a men's maximum-security prison, but she says even there it held true. "I was working with people who had done heinous, heinous crimes, and I was seeing Light in them and was looking forward to seeing them every week." She adds, "It is my responsibility to go through life looking for that spark of holiness in someone. If I don't find it, it's not because it's not there; it's because I haven't done my job."

Fear can be one of the major obstacles to seeing the good in others, but tapping into compassion may be particularly important when we are afraid because, as the Dalai Lama explained in the last chapter, compassion often brings us strength and courage. I recall my junior year in college when I started receiving obscene phone calls. The first time I was so surprised, it took me a minute to hang up. A week later the young man called again.

He said he had been watching me and knew I had cut my hair. "I'm going to rape you," he said before I gasped and slammed down the phone. Not only was he right about my haircut, twice in a row he had caught me alone in my room, making me wonder if he was watching to see when my roommate was out. I started glancing over my shoulder at night and pulling the shades. Then I heard that a young woman down the hall from me was getting similar calls, so I went to hear her story. She was in her dorm room telling a small audience about the young man's daily, violent threats. She demonstrated how she dropped the phone and screamed every time he called. Suddenly I realized this was exactly what he wanted—our fear and the sense of power it gave him. That's why he called the other woman more often than he called me. Her screams made her more fun. I suddenly saw him as a lonely, troubled soul—someone to pity, rather than fear.

The next time the man called, he began with the rape threat, but this time I was not afraid. "I'm concerned about your mental health," I said calmly. There was silence on the other end. "You must be very sad or disturbed to be making calls like this. Did you know the university offers a free counseling service?" There was still no response, so I gave simple directions to the counseling office on the other side of campus. "I hope they can help you," I concluded sincerely. This time, he hung up and never called back.

While you cannot change anyone else, acting out of your best self can make it more likely that they will change their own behavior. There is no guarantee, of course, and certainly no excuse for blaming the victims of violence. Still, many people have found that tapping the good in themselves is the best way to bring out the good in others. Throughout his writing, Thich Nhat Hanh tells many such stories of people becoming mindful of their own anger, turning to compassion, and that in turn opening someone else to a new way of relating. We can't fake this kind of change in ourselves, pretending to be compassionate in the hopes of manipulating other people, but knowing that it might improve our relationships can be an incentive to work on ourselves. In *The Art of Power*, Hanh notes, "There are occasions when the lack of understanding between you and another is really there." Instead of worrying about the misunderstanding or trying to change someone else's mind, Hanh advises that we remain loving and think positively. "Your value will reveal itself to the people around you. It may take a few days or several weeks, it may even take years. But if you know who you are, you don't have to suffer anymore." Your beautiful thoughts and actions "will transform everything else."

Remaining loving is not the same as becoming a doormat or keeping silent about things that you believe are wrong. Thich Nhat Hanh himself has spoken out against war many times, though he does so with compassion for even the most powerful perpetrators of violence. Ironically, confronting people with love can be more effective than confronting them in a spirit of anger or self-righteousness. A funny series of incidents made me realize the difference. It started one night when I walked up some steps with a friend, and the man in front of us dropped some papers. "Excuse me, sir," I said as I stooped to pick up the papers, "I think you dropped these." It wasn't until I was handing the papers to the man, who looked deeply embarrassed and contrite, that I realized they were trash. My friend, who had realized from

THE WISDOM TO KNOW THE DIFFERENCE

the beginning that the man was simply littering, was stifling a smirk. "I can't believe you did that!" he said afterward. But I had been sincere in my desire to be helpful. It was only afterward that I was pleased with myself for shaming a litterbug.

I have always been annoyed by littering. Since the "Excuse me, sir" line had worked so well once, I decided to try it the next two times I spotted someone tossing their trash on the sidewalk. Of course, in these cases I knew what I was doing, feigning sincerity, and the results were not nearly so satisfying. On both occasions I was called a word I'd rather not put in print, evoking anger and defensiveness in the litterbug, rather than remorse. Perhaps the first man was different from the second two, more prone to guilt, but I don't think that was it. I believe the difference was in my attitude. When I was feeling like a self-righteous know-it-all, my actions were less effective. It is certainly true, from the other side, that I am less likely to change my behavior when someone I perceive to be self-righteous tells me what to do, like one environmentalist who tried to shame me for using a disposable cup while I was traveling with two children. Many other people have inspired me to try to reduce my environmental footprint, but they have done it through setting a positive example and encouraging my efforts, not through scolding. It's a lesson I have to keep remembering, since I know I am prone to being judgmental myself.

Musician Will Brock used to think, "I'm right, I'm right, I'm right" when arguing with people who disagreed with him. Instead of exchanging ideas, they hurled ideas at each other. Now he consciously tries to say, " 'I want to hear what you have to say, really want to check you out.' So, suddenly that whole trench warfare thing goes away, and we're sitting and discussing ideas for real. You don't have a choice but to check out the fact that you're being heard, and the more you feel like you're being heard, the more open you are to hearing someone else's thing," he explains. Will notes that when he is willing to really listen to another person, they become more willing to listen to his point of view, thus helping them both find common ground.

Sometimes one person's attitude has a contagious effect. In the last chapter, Park Dong-Sun described how his life was transformed after meeting the Zen master whose mindfulness inspired Dong-Sun to quit drinking and change his life. Likewise, Father Michael Doyle was changed by hearing the story of the British mother who advised her son to "always be good to the people." As Joan Countryman said of most teachers, the mother never had a glimmer of her influence, though her words have continued to have a ripple effect through the many people who have been influenced by Father Doyle.

Often the effect we have on each other is mutual. In chapter 2, Eileen Smith talked about the meeting of God in one another that happens during the meal program of her nonprofit, Face to Face. Although Eileen believes this can happen in small and ordinary ways, she once had a dramatic experience of it as a Catholic sister visiting AIDS patients in the early, hopeless years of the disease. One week Eileen visited a poor woman named London, who had been brought to the hospital from prison. London was so weak, she was slumped over her food tray, despite being tied to her chair. "I'll never forget it," recalls Eileen. "She was trying to navigate this spoon of oatmeal into her mouth, and it was just kind of oozing out of her mouth and down her front.

I was getting heaves watching her." London only had one good eye, which seemed unable to focus. After speaking to her for several minutes with no response, Eileen suggested they pray the Our Father together. "So I held her hands, and as I said the Our Father, her whole posture changed. She started to sit up. It was like pouring water on a plant. Every time I water a plant, I think of her. Somewhere in her memory, she had a grandparent or a parent or mentor who prayed with her, and this Our Father was just familiar to her. By the time I left, she was sitting upright; she was focused. We really connected, and I was so happy." As Eileen prepared to leave, London asked her for a kiss, a memory that still makes Eileen teary.

Through her compassion and prayer, Eileen was able to nourish London. The next time she saw London, Eileen had an even more profound experience. She had been thinking about London all week, but when she arrived at the hospital, London was stretched out in bed, emaciated and unconscious. Eileen tried talking to her but got no response. A few minutes later, as Eileen was making her rounds, London died. "I went in, and there was a nurse sitting on the bed bathing London with her head kind of propped up. I had the most profound experience of the *pietà*— the image of Jesus being laid in the arms of his mother after being taken down from the cross. It was so real," Eileen recalls with emotion. "I never had such a close experience of God. I just knew that London, the crucified Christ, had been taken off her cross. I could hardly move, it was so sacred and so deep." Eileen says that because of her Catholic faith and her understanding of liberation theology, this image of God suffering with and through God's people had special meaning for her and strengthened her commitment to continue serving people in need. "Most people didn't even know that London lived or died," concludes Eileen. "I feel like I've been entrusted with her memory."

We cannot create or force the kind of mystical vision that Eileen experienced, but we can prepare ourselves to be open to such moments when they occur. Eileen's willingness to be present and compassionate—even when she felt disgusted by an emaciated, drooling woman who seemed to be unreachable—opened her to the grace that followed. By trying to "connect" she was able to be a conduit of love, to which London clearly responded. But the encounter nurtured Eileen, as well, even though London surely had no idea that she had strengthened the sister's sense of calling. Most of us have no idea of what ripples we've created, whether positive or negative, but as surely as a boat leaves a wake, our actions have an effect that may continue out of our sight. We may open a door for someone else, as Joan put it, and never learn whether or not they went through it.

Just as acting out of our best selves can prompt others to do the same, acting out of fear and mistrust can prompt the very responses we dread. It is another case of the law of attraction, creating a dynamic that draws the worst out of other people, rather than the best. I once observed a painful incident at a six-year-old's birthday party held at a local arboretum. The middle-aged white woman who was the staff person for the arboretum was gruff with the mostly white girls who were at the party, but when we went for a hike and encountered a group of young black boys from the surrounding urban neighborhood, she became outright hostile. She accused the boys of being up to no good, despite my impression that they were just playing by the pond. After she made several unsuccessful attempts to catch a tadpole to show the birthday girls, one of the boys caught a tadpole in his basin and offered it to her, but she accused him of trying to hurt the tadpole. Clearly hurt himself, the boy dumped the tadpole back. A few minutes later, she accused the boys of trying to steal the bucket she had left by the edge of the pond, even though the boys had their own basin to scoop the water. After she confiscated their basin, supposedly to teach them a lesson, the boys jumped on their bikes, rode back to the arboretum office, and stole the woman's butterfly nets, thus living down to her expectations of them.

When I suggested to the woman that her treatment of the boys had initiated the negative dynamic between them, she wouldn't hear of it. She couldn't imagine that treating them with respect could have brought a different result, though I kept imagining how the afternoon might have gone if she had praised the boy who had caught the tadpole and encouraged his enthusiasm for nature. This is not to suggest that you are responsible whenever someone steals from you or treats you poorly, just that you are not always as powerless as you feel. Especially when you are dealing with children, changing your own attitude and perspective is usually the best way to influence another's behavior.

"You can get rid of just about any behavior by rewarding behaviors that are incompatible with it," states Alan Kazdin, a leader in the field of child psychology. Kazdin, whose many titles include director of the Yale Parenting Center and Child Conduct Clinic, has developed a detailed manual to help parents eliminate aggression and tantrums in children. But here is the kicker: the parents have to change their own behavior first. "There's a gentle deception in what we do," he explains. "The parents think they're here to fix the child, but we're training the parents." First, the parents must learn to remain calm themselves, since studies show that bellowing threats doesn't work. Parents must also be very specific about what they want the child to do and lavish praise when the child complies. "Seventy-eight percent of the time the children get much better," says Kazdin, though he adds that "even the best-behaved child only does what he's told about eighty percent of the time."

Kazdin's studies on how to change children illustrate many principles that can be applied to your encounters with any people you might hope to influence. First, stay calm. Control yourself before you try to change anyone else. Then say what you want, and be specific. Also, praise and thank others. Finally, accept that you still won't always get what you want. These rules for parents sound like the wisdom to know the difference in a nutshell. Although what you do has an impact, accepting that you will never get people to do what you want a hundred percent of the time is an important lesson in accepting the things you cannot change. As an Internet version of the Serenity Prayer puts it:

God, grant me serenity to accept the people I cannot change,
Courage to change the one I can change,
And the wisdom to know it's me.

ACCEPTING THAT YOU CAN'T
CHANGE OTHER PEOPLE

As a parent and as a teacher, it's part of my job to tell other people what to do. As a citizen, I lobby my legislators with letters and e-mails asking them to vote for bills I support. When it's election season, I go out knocking on doors to encourage my neighbors to vote. Even when I am trying to influence others, however, I know I can't control them. I can't *make* my neighbors vote or my students learn. I can only do my best to motivate them. Even as a parent, there are limits to how much power I have over my children. I can open a door for them, as Joan Countryman says, but I can't make them go through. In fact, parenthood is the experience that has taught me the most about accepting that I can't change other people, though I confess I haven't always accepted it with serenity.

Accepting that we don't totally control our children is especially difficult. After all, as parents it is our job to keep them safe and healthy and to teach them not to pick their noses in public. A certain exercise of control is called for, especially near traffic. However, as any parent of a toddler knows, guiding often works better than forcing. When I had an eighteen-month-old, my greatest power was in anticipating the right moment: offering food not too soon, when she wasn't hungry, but not too late, when she was cranky from hunger. I could get a dangerous object out of her hands, not by grabbing it or prying her fingers open, but by offering a toy to distract her. The dance between guiding and forcing has gotten trickier now that my daughter is a preteen, but I am still helped by the Taoist advice I read as a new parent: "Instead of putting effort into making something happen become aware of what is really occurring. Look for the forces that are at work" and ally oneself with those forces. This strategy, mentioned in chapter 3, is called *wu wei*, often translated as "non-doing" or "the art of letting be."

Wu wei does not imply apathetic passivity, but going with the flow, working with the nature of things. It suggests that doing less is often more effective than aggressive action, as in aikido—the martial art that grew out of Taoism—where a person does not try to oppose an opponent's energy, but instead moves with the opponent so that he (or she) wastes energy, eventually defeating themselves. When my children were small, I often defeated myself, interpreting normal preschool behavior as a personal affront, thus making everything into a battle of wills. I was much more effective when I inadvertently followed Alan Kazdin's advice, keeping calm myself and asking for what I wanted in a positive way. When I expected the best from my children, I was more likely to get it.

Kazdin's advice can apply to adults as well as children. Once, when I was training for a promotion in the canvass organization I mentioned in the last chapter, I was sent to work for a month in another state. When I arrived, a woman who had just undergone the same training I was beginning warned me about one of the women I would be working with. "She's a total control freak," she said angrily. "She was always trying to do part of my job for me." The woman who was leaving felt undermined by the other woman's help with a relatively minor administrative task and spent the whole month in a power struggle with her. Intuitively

I suspected the "control freak" was needy, rather than malicious, and that the woman who felt undermined was projecting her own insecurities. The first day I told the "control freak" that since I was new, I hoped I could rely on her experience in the region and asked her to do the task my predecessor had felt threatened to give up. She was thrilled to feel needed and became one of the biggest supporters of my leadership.

There are times when you should stand up for what you believe in or set limits with your children, but that is different from getting locked in a petty power struggle that is about egos and emotions more than substance. Unfortunately it is often hard to see the difference when you are in the midst of it. Trying to stay centered in your best self can help.

For Sally Jergesen, thinking about what is in the best interest of her son has helped her navigate the messy waters of divorce. As she and her ex-husband continue to negotiate child care arrangements, she is trying to let go of her desire to control him, while standing up for herself when he backs out of agreements they made in mediation. "That's been a bit of a process," she notes, admitting that their negotiations often turn into power plays between the two of them. "One of my concerns is, if I hassle him too much about the fact that he's not spending much time with our son, then he's going to feel only guilt and obligation toward him. I can't make him want to be a good parent," she notes with sadness. As she tries to "go with the flow a bit more," Sally holds onto the message of self-help books she has read: "You can't control another's actions, and the more you try to control another person and tell them, 'You're making a bad decision. You're doing this wrong,' the harder it will be for them to take responsibility for their own actions and do the right thing," says Sally. "Letting go doesn't mean that you're letting someone walk all over you, but sometimes if you let go, the outcome you want is more likely to happen anyway," she concludes.

Sally is right about the power of letting go. When I was single, in my early thirties, and hoping to get married, I had a rather sudden realization that I couldn't *make* love happen and that my attempts to make men love me hadn't been working out very well. I had to simply be open and trust I would meet someone if and when I was meant to. I noticed how contrary this attitude was to the advice offered on the self-help shelves, which were full of books like *How to Get Married in a Year or Less* and *Guerrilla Dating Tactics*. Yearning for a different approach, I interviewed women I respected about how they entered committed relationships and was struck by how many of them met the person they eventually married soon *after* they gave up looking. In contrast, the women who tried to pressure men into marrying them always ended up disappointed, although sometimes after the wedding. Hearing these stories helped me let go of my own anxiety about finding a partner, which was particularly helpful since I had become attracted to a man who was a Roman Catholic priest.

As I mentioned in chapter 3, Tom and I had become friends after I let go of my plans to move to the mountains and accepted that I would be at Pendle Hill for another semester. He was there on sabbatical to discern whether God was calling him out of the priesthood. Unlike me, Tom is very patient with the discernment process. He took more than a year, including a thirty-day silent retreat, a semester at a spiritual study center, a temporary assignment in a new parish, reading, paying attention to dreams, talking to spiritual directors, a lot of prayer, and waiting. Midway through his discernment process, I began to have feelings for him, though it was clear I could not act on them until he had made his decision. I just had to wait to see if my sense that he might be "the one" was correct. The waiting was difficult because his decision was not something I could control, though it taught me a greater trust in the Divine. While I was writing a book that was originally about finding peace in being single, Tom decided to leave the priesthood, and the relationship began that led to our marriage.

Although letting go, in my case, did lead to what I most wanted, it doesn't always happen that way. Realizing that you can't control other people is often a difficult lesson, as Yvonne Thompson notes: "You can't control them. You can't make them love you. There's a whole lot of can'ts." Now nearly eighty, she adds with a sigh, "That took me forever to learn." For Yvonne, the hardest person to accept was her own mother. "I've always been big and awkward with these broad shoulders, big hands, and big feet," she says. In contrast, her twin sister and her other siblings were very dainty, like their mother. Yvonne felt like Cinderella, the girl in the corner with the cinders while her siblings were doted on. "I couldn't understand why if you were little you were loved, and if you were big you weren't," recalls Yvonne, a naturally affectionate person who was also hurt that her mother wasn't more demonstrative. "I was very unhappy with my mother, very, very, very unhappy with her. It wasn't until years after she died that I learned that if you want oranges, you don't go where they grow apples. What I wanted, my mother did not have. That was a great lesson for me," she explains. "I can no longer blame my mother. That's what she knew." Today Yvonne feels more at peace with herself than she has for most of her life, which makes it easier for her to accept other people, including her grown children, who do not always make the choices she wishes they would.

Often it is the people closest to you who are the hardest to accept. Maybe you want love and feel disappointed and hurt when it doesn't come in the form you wish. Maybe you are afraid that your loved one's behavior will inconvenience or reflect poorly on you. Maybe you simply want power in the relationship and convince yourself that you are acting in the other's best interest. Or maybe you really do want what is best for them and are convinced that you know what that is. In any case, conflicts with parents, children, and spouses are often the most challenging and painful.

Sometimes it takes hindsight to realize that you do not necessarily know what is best for those you love. Ro'Bin White Morton offers a great example of this, recalling that she tried to talk her son out of leaving New Orleans a week early for his freshman year of college. He ignored her advice and missed Hurricane Katrina as a result. "Talk about God!" Ro'Bin exclaims. She points out that sometimes one person might be listening to God, but their loved ones don't realize it. In fact, the summer before Katrina, Ro'Bin felt compelled to spend hours typing up much of her poetry and e-mailing it to herself. At that point her son thought she was being absurd, but in hindsight Ro'Bin says God was guiding her to save her writing from the coming flood, which destroyed all the work that had not been e-mailed.

Realizing that other people can hear God's guidance as well

as or better than you may help you to let go of your desire to tell them what to do. As Joan Countryman said of her children, they have their own lives. During our interview, she referenced the chapter "On Children" from Kahlil Gibran's *The Prophet*, which says, in part: "You are the bows from which your children as living arrows are sent forth. The archer sees the mark upon the path of the infinite, and He bends you with His might that His arrows may go swift and far." Trusting that there is an archer guiding your children or others you care about can help you to let go of your desire to steer them, even when you are convinced that you know which way they should go. Instead of giving up on people you care about, you can get out of the way and let God work changes that you could not accomplish yourself.

Trusting God has certainly been important to Matthew Cole as he has watched his fourteen-year-old son begin to use drugs and get in trouble with the law. Matthew has also been helped by "The Three Cs" cited in Al-Anon, the organization that supports the family members of alcoholics: " 'I didn't cause it; I can't control it; and I can't cure it.' I'm powerless over my son and his choices," explains Matthew. "I certainly am not causing his problems now, if I ever caused them. I'm definitely not in control, and I can't cure him. All I can do is love him and let him know that, and let him know what my boundaries are. I'm not powerless over how I respond and how I relate." Staying centered and sober himself is one of the best things Matthew can do for his son, though even this is no guarantee. He can't even control his son's home environment since Matthew's ex-wife has custody of their two children. Letting go of his desire to control his ex-wife's behavior has been another challenge.

Matthew refers to his divorce as "a great challenge and a great gift" that has tested his ability to surrender. He explains that in hindsight his marriage was a big mistake. "I was three months sober, and she was four months sober," he recalls, adding that the conventional wisdom in AA is that you should avoid romantic or sexual relationships for the first year in the program. Although Matthew did manage to stay sober during twelve years of an increasingly hostile marriage, he felt pulled away from both AA and his faith community. He felt angry and found himself yelling at their two children. Because he wanted to keep the family together, he thinks he ignored signs that his wife's behavior was unhealthy, possibly addictive again. "I was just consumed with wanting to control the family and keep it together," he recalls, saying that he tried unsuccessfully to get the family into counseling. "At some point, I just knew I needed to get out of there. I needed help." His greatest regret was that he wasn't able to take the children with him.

When you are in the midst of it, you may not see that your attempts to control other people can facilitate the very situations you fear. Pushing an ex-husband to spend more time with his child may inadvertently push him away. Trying to keep a family together at all costs may exacerbate problems that need to be dealt with. Battling a coworker to prove your authority may actually undermine it. This does not mean that you should have no boundaries or let other people walk all over you. Instead, when you stop trying to control someone else, you may be better able to discern what you are called to do yourself.

DISCERNMENT AND LISTENING

Figuring out how to stand up for yourself or others you care about without becoming judgmental or controlling can be a difficult journey. It may begin with a vague feeling that something isn't right, as it did for a singer whom I'll call Laura. Her work was going well, bringing her a series of profitable recording contracts, but Laura had a nagging feeling that her manager wasn't really looking out for her interests. She had moved into pop, while he specialized in jazz, but she ignored the growing sense that she should change managers because she didn't want to hurt his feelings. He had helped her get her first break back when she was unknown, and now, as a successful woman in her forties, she didn't want anyone to think she was disloyal or becoming a diva. Acknowledging her fear of what other people would think, she complained to friends, "I'm such a girl!"

Then, in the midst of a complex contract negotiation, the manager overlooked some important details. When Laura asked him about it, he casually mentioned that he had been spending too much time on the Internet. Laura felt angry, as well as disrespected. Talking with other women helped her realize that she had in fact told her manager what she needed from him many times, and that he had shown on numerous occasions that he was just unable to give it to her. She could either accept his substandard work or change managers, which she ultimately realized was the only way to be true to herself. Still, Laura wanted to honor the friendship they had developed, so she broke the news to him in the most respectful way she could manage. Rather than tell him her decision in an e-mail or letter, she scheduled a phone call for a time when she knew it would be easiest for him to hear difficult news. "I want to take the high road," she explained to friends. Although the actual conversation was very painful, at the end of the process she felt liberated. She is now signed with a manager whose skills are a much better fit with where she is in her career. Her old manager may still be angry about losing her lucrative business, but Laura has realized that she is not responsible for his feelings, though she did try to listen to them with compassion. Coming to this clarity was a difficult journey, but she learned that sometimes you have to do what you believe is right, even if it is frightening or painful.

When you are trying to decide when to act and when to let go or wait, it may be helpful to remember all the work we have discussed in the previous chapters—recognizing your social conditioning, letting go of denial and anger, centering into your best self. For Laura, the phrase "I'm such a girl!" was a way of recognizing her tendency as a woman to feel overly responsible for other people's feelings. Because she shared her struggle with friends, they were able to remind her of all the times she had told her manager what she needed, breaking through her denial that things weren't that bad. Scheduling a time to talk with him, rather than reacting in an emotional moment, gave her a chance to work through her own emotions and "take the high road." None of this made the phone call easy, but it led to a better result than if Laura had either stifled her anger or lashed out impulsively.

Laura was right to ask for what she wanted from her manager before giving up on him and severing their business relationship.

But as she learned, sometimes asking politely is not enough. In such cases, we must accept that we cannot force someone to change, while evaluating the options available to us.

Peter Warrington had been an obstetrician/gynecologist for twelve years though he was thinking of changing medical fields at the time we spoke, something he has since done. Now he is retrained as a geriatric specialist, but in our interview he talked about the role of obstetrician, where influencing a mother's behavior is often part of the job. Pensive and soft-spoken, Peter noted that before the women's movement, obstetricians spoke more authoritatively, with less regard for the mother's opinion. He is glad the culture has changed to become more respectful of women's choices, but he notes there are still times when a doctor needs to tell people what is best for them or their children.

"I have a pregnant woman now who is a heroine addict," says Peter, noting that he is giving her methadone, which is much less risky for the baby than street heroine. "I'm quite sure she's not being truthful with us when we ask if she's using substances other than what we're giving her," he says. Peter has tried to convey to her the danger of doing street drugs, but he has learned over the years that if he is too accusatory, she might not continue with the prenatal care her baby needs. Because of such experiences, he has developed a softer approach. "I'm going to try to take care of her as best I can and then try to step up the intervention when she's in labor and after birth," he explains.

Not that many of us end up in Peter's position—making life-or-death decisions for the unborn child of a heroin addict—but many adults face the challenge of trying to discern how much to try to change the behavior of adult children or aging parents.

When you are worried about someone you care about, praying and listening to your inner guidance may be particularly important. You may not be able to rationally predict what will be best for the situation; you can only do your best to sense how you are called to act. As my own mother aged, the most difficult question I faced was when to respect her desire to refuse medical care and when to intervene.

Always a petite woman, my mother was down to eighty-five pounds as she approached her eighty-second birthday. One day she felt weak and stopped eating altogether. For days I urged her to see her doctor, but she refused. I suspected she had pneumonia again, a risk of her chronic lung condition, but she responded that pneumonia wouldn't be the worst way to go. Later I realized that she feared her weight loss was a sign of cancer and thought that dying of pneumonia might be quicker and less painful than death from cancer. But I couldn't stand watching what seemed like a slow and not very well-informed suicide. "At least find out what's wrong with you," I urged. "You can always refuse treatment if you don't want to fight it, but you should at least know what you have." She refused.

After my mother had been in bed about a week, I had a startling dream in which I was phoning her apartment. I heard the phone pulled off the receiver, but there was no voice on the other end. I woke up, convinced that my mother would die if I didn't get her care soon, and clear that I was meant to take action. I drove to her apartment before the sun was fully up and told her firmly that I was taking her to the hospital. This time she gave her weak assent.

It turned out that my mother's fear of cancer was unfounded.

It was pneumonia, which was treatable with antibiotics. Though she never regained her previous strength or independence, my mother did live another year during which she was able to say goodbye to those she loved, something she might not have been able to do if she had died from the pneumonia. We were able to reconcile most of the rough spots in our relationship, and she was able to grow closer to her grandchildren.

My mother had always taken care of her health, lifting weights and swimming three times a week until she was eighty-one. She believed in health food long before it was fashionable. In fact, good food had always been one of her great pleasures, one that was spoiled by the antibiotics she continued to take after coming home from the hospital. Her appetite was something she couldn't afford to lose, as her weight continued to evaporate even after several months at home. Eventually she decided to give up the antibiotics and ask for hospice services. This time I felt her decision was well-informed and well-considered. I didn't try to change her mind.

What was the difference between her two decisions? The first time, when she refused to go to the doctor, she was operating totally out of fear, with no information about her actual condition. She admitted later that she was practically killing herself, but "didn't have the nerve" to go through with it. After all, she was Catholic and didn't believe that suicide was right. She would not have died at peace. Meanwhile I felt irresponsible letting her waste away, knowing that doctors could probably help her. When my mother chose to refuse further medical intervention several months later, the circumstances were very different. She made the decision when her mind wasn't muddled by dehydration or pneumonia. She had endured repeated medical tests to diagnose her weight loss, had consulted several doctors, and understood how her lung disease was likely to progress. She wasn't choosing between life and death. She was choosing between death at home, where she could enjoy Java Chip ice cream unhampered by appetite-suppressing antibiotics, and death in an institution that might lengthen the quantity of her time while diminishing the quality.

However, even as I lay out the logical differences between the two situations, I realize that isn't really it. For me, the real difference was that the first time I felt led to intervene, and the second time I did not. My dramatic dream was confirmed by the peace and clarity I felt when I arrived at my mother's apartment to take her to the hospital. Several months later when my mother asked for hospice, I felt at peace again. Although watching her decline was painful, I never had a sense that I was called to do more than care for her and respect her wishes.

Knowing how you are called to act in regard to other people is not always easy, but the same rules apply as in other types of discernment. You need to make space in your life to listen, paying attention to your own agendas and motivations and sifting them out so you can sense the guidance of the Spirit within you. This can be particularly difficult when you feel strongly about the other person or when the situation ignites your own anxiety, as the impending death of a loved one often does. Being honest with yourself about how you feel can help you sort out the difference between how you feel and how you are called to act.

Dr. Dan Gottlieb—a psychologist, author, and radio talk

show host—says that we have to be particularly attentive to our own emotions and suffering when we are trying to help someone else. "Both overinvolvement and underinvolvement come from anxiety," he explains, noting that women often err on the side of intervening in a loved one's problems, while men are more likely to err on the side of not intervening. To find the right balance, he advises, "Know your anxiety. Tolerate your anxiety, and love carefully and fully both of those people in that interaction. And then discern." For Dan love is the most important factor, making sure your behavior is truly motivated by love rather than by your own need.

A family therapist for nearly forty years, Dan acknowledges that there are times when people need someone else's perspective, particularly in the face of depression, which is often recognized by others before it is acknowledged by the depressed person. In his own life, he recalls going to visit his daughter when she was twenty and "out of control" in so many ways that Dan thought her life was in jeopardy. He arranged professional help for her and insisted she get treatment. Although he was unusually forceful in this situation, he says he was also respectful and loving. Still, it wasn't until she took responsibility for it a few years later that her life really changed. He warns that we can't rush people in this process. When he needed therapy himself after a car accident that left him paralyzed and later clinically depressed, he said he had to choose a therapist very carefully because most of them wanted to help him too fast and give him advice. "I quote very often Sheldon Kopp, who wrote a book that I consider my Bible as a therapist called *If You Meet the Buddha on the Road, Kill Him*. One of the things he says is that one of the most painful parts of love is tolerating your own helplessness in the face of a loved one's suffering."

As a therapist, Dan finds that much of his job is to love people and help them tolerate their fear and helplessness in the face of the things they cannot change. "I usually smile and in so many words, I say, 'Just sit. We'll figure out what we can change and what we have to live with, but we'll start assuming that we have to accept all of it, and we can change none of it, and we'll live there for a long time. And then we will start to explore what we'd like to change.'" Dan has found that sitting with people, listening, and simply loving them is more likely to cure them than anything else.

Deep listening is a skill, but also a spiritual practice. To listen nondefensively, to really listen to someone, requires you to tap into your best self. You have to put aside your masks, your insecurities, and your projections, and just be present. This kind of listening is often a tremendous gift to the person who is speaking. For all the time we spend talking on cell phones and chatting via e-mail, most of us don't have that many occasions when another person gives us their undivided attention. Really being listened to often frees a person to let go of anger, though you can't force this to happen. In fact, people can usually tell if you are listening with an agenda, even if you don't realize it yourself. If you are planning what you are going to say in response while someone else is speaking, that's a clue that you are not really listening. Letting go of your desire to respond and be right is not always easy—in fact, it is often hard!—though real listening can actually change people much more effectively than talking at them. Learning to "reflect" about things—saying something like, "What I heard you say was . . ."—can get you out of the

THE WISDOM TO KNOW THE DIFFERENCE

habit of defending yourself or arguing, though it won't work if you try to use it as a new tool for manipulating people. They can tell when your listening is sincere.

LISTENING EXERCISE

Pick a time when you are going to practice listening to one other person with one hundred percent of your attention. You may want to try this with a friend, where you take turns speaking for five uninterrupted minutes each about something important to you. If you don't have a partner who wants to do this as an exercise, try concentrated listening in some other circumstance where someone wants your attention—a spouse, a coworker, a friend, or an aging parent. Even if you think of yourself as a generally good listener, you may be surprised to realize how often other thoughts float through your head when someone else is speaking. Think of this time as a kind of meditation practice, where you are gently pushing aside any judgments or thoughts about what you want to say in response. Just sit in a comfortable position and focus all your attention on the speaker. Try to understand what they are saying, as if your life depends on it. Pay attention to the person's body language and the emotions that seem to be behind the words. When the person has finished speaking, you may want to reflect about what you've heard, if it feels appropriate to the situation.

Ideally, deep listening will become a habit, but to cultivate this habit you need to consciously decide to do it. Because it is much more difficult than it sounds—especially if the person is saying something that triggers a strong emotional reaction in you—it is good to begin practicing in situations that are not too emotionally charged. For example, if you can listen well when a friend is frustrated about work, you may be better able to listen when a loved one is frustrated with you. It is in such situations that deep listening is most helpful, enabling you to understand a problem rather than just react to it defensively. You don't have to wait for the perfect peaceful moment, however. Use whatever opportunities present themselves. If you are actively listening in a situation where you simply must respond, that's okay. Let the other person feel heard first. Then, as Will Brock pointed out, it will be easier for them to hear you.

Teacher Marcelle Martin learned the power of listening in the difficult relationship she described in chapter 3. As the pain in her heart prompted her to be true to herself, she learned to listen nondefensively to what her partner had to say and speak honestly without it being an attack on him. This experience has helped her in many situations since, including as a teacher. "When someone comes to me with a complaint, I'm much better at just listening and reflecting over it without defensiveness. I still might have anxiety about it, but at least I've realized that it is safe to hear it. And I've often noticed that just hearing it and reflecting over it defuses a lot of difficulty in the situation." Marcelle observes: "Relationships with other people are an intense spiritual practice, if you see them that way."

Indeed, the spiritual practice of accepting other people can help us learn to accept all the other things we cannot change, the subject of the next chapter.

Queries

Who do you most wish to change? Why?

What anxieties does this person arouse in you?

Have you ever tried really listening to this person?

Can you see that of God in them?

Can you see how your actions influence others?

Are there attitudes you could change in yourself that might help bring out the best in others?

Are you more likely to overintervene in someone else's problems or ignore a situation where you should intervene?

Have you ever felt divine guidance regarding your relationships with others?

Six

LETTING GO OF OUTCOMES

When asked about letting go, Dr. Dan Gottlieb looks at his stiff hands, which were paralyzed in a car accident twenty-nine years ago. "I can't clutch," he says, lifting his arm off the side of his wheelchair. "I can't hold on to anything. So maybe it was twenty-nine years ago that I was forced to learn to let go." Before the accident that broke his spine, Dan was married with two young children and was the director of an outpatient substance abuse program. "Right after the accident I felt everything you would expect: despair, anger, helplessness, rage, grief, and breathtaking shame," he recalls. "I was so ashamed of what I couldn't do, so ashamed of how I looked. It was agony." Dan says he couldn't tolerate the truth that his legs would never feel again, so one day he called a nurse into his room and begged her to break his leg, just in the hope that he would feel pain.

"It seemed every day after the accident the doctors were

coming in and telling me something else I would have to live with the rest of my life: paralysis, skin breakouts, bladder infections, bowel problems, and on and on." With so much out of his control, Dan clung to whatever he could. For example, the night before he was scheduled for fusion surgery, a technician came in with a razor to shave his beard. "I said, 'No, I've had it for fifteen years. You're not shaving my beard.' " The technician explained that the surgeons would be cutting through his neck and needed the area clean, but Dan refused. When the technician couldn't convince him, a nurse and then the head nurse were called. "I said, 'I will lie in this fucking bed and die before you cut my beard off!' " The doctors were called at home on Sunday night and eventually only a patch of Dan's beard was shaved. "I would not accept it," he says with a smile, noting that he still tries to control whatever he can. "Stuff that is unimportant to others is important to me because there is so much I can't control," he explains.

For the last twenty years Dan has been using his writing, his radio show, and his practice to help others who are clinging too tightly to control. His tone is warm with compassion born of his own experience. "So what prevents us from letting go?" he asks. "Anxiety, that's all. And what lets us let go? The opposite of anxiety, which is faith. You know, in the Bible, when God says to Abraham in the Hebrew words *lekh lekha*, the traditional interpretation of that is 'Leave your father's house.' But a rabbi told me that the literal translation is 'Leave what is familiar.' In my case, I got pushed out of what was familiar at every level, so I was desperately looking for things to grasp for safety." Along with his mobility and independence, Dan lost his best friend, who couldn't handle seeing Dan in a wheelchair, and his wife, who left him a few years after the accident. In the following years, his mother, his sister, and his ex-wife all died. "Everything I grasped for I lost," he recalls. "And then the clinical depression hit, which was far worse in hindsight than the quadriplegia itself. After the depression, I think I started to learn what I needed to learn about life," although he adds that he was probably gradually learning it all along.

Raised Jewish and recently reengaged with a synagogue, Dan found learning about Buddhism very helpful, especially the insight that it is clinging to our picture of how we think life should be that makes us suffer. He was forced to let go of his picture of himself as someone who *should* be able to walk and who *should* have a wife. He says that his own experience is unique only in the details and that all people have essentially the same struggle. He tells the story of a friend who had a picture in her head of the kind of family she wanted. "She got married, but the guy was mean-spirited, and then he got ill, and that wasn't the picture." After he died, she dated other men, but none were what she had in mind. Then she thought her daughter's marriage might make her happy, but her son-in-law didn't fit the picture, either. "She says she's had a miserable life," says Dan. "Why? It was because of the picture, and that's all. It was the picture that ruined her life." He says that as long as we are striving to make our lives fit some perfect ideal, we will be anxious and won't be present to the lives we have. Practicing mindfulness (which Thich Nhat Hanh described in chapter 2) helped Dan learn to accept the life he has and feel grateful for it.

It also helped Dan to recognize that suffering is part of life and that he is more resilient than he could have imagined. "It was at my wife's funeral, which was six months after my mother's funeral," he recalls. There was no clear place for an ex-spouse, so Dan felt alone watching his daughters grieve with his ex-wife's family. "It was agony for me," he recalls. "I'm leaving the cemetery by myself, and I'm passing the line of limousines where all the mourners were, seeing my father-in-law and all the suffering. I looked to the heavens as I was leaving, and I said, 'I can't take any more pain.' And the voice back said, 'Yes, you can. You just don't want to.' " Dan explains that much of our anxiety is about wanting to avoid suffering. If we can acknowledge and tolerate this fear, we can gradually feel more peace.

Now in his early sixties with recurrent bladder infections due to his paralysis, Dan has been thinking about the ultimate limit we have to accept: death. Because he has lost several people close to him and has had several severe illnesses himself, death is not unfamiliar to him, though he has recently come to greater peace about it. Previous times when he thought he might die, he wondered, "Is this it? Is this the time?" He felt scared and then relieved when the illness was over. "Nothing changed," he observes. Then in the past year, when he got an infection that the doctors said they couldn't cure and he thought he might be dying, he realized that he wasn't scared anymore. "I was sad, but I wasn't clutching to my life. One day I wondered, 'Well, if I do survive, do I want to do anything differently with my life?' And my answer was no. I would like to slow down a drop, but that wasn't a big deal. I don't want to change anything. I learned a lot from that answer. I'm living my life, and it's a blessing," he concludes.

The Process of Letting Go

Dan's story illustrates that letting go is not a glib mantra or a quick fix, but a gradual process of accepting the things we cannot change, starting with ourselves and our own painful emotions. Accepting that life will bring difficulties can help us let go of our anxiety and our picture of how we think things should be. Accepting that our lives will eventually end can also, paradoxically, bring us the peace to make the most of the lives we have. Whether or not we ever face anything as dramatic as a paralyzing car accident, following Dan's example of accepting our emotions and accepting our mortality can help us move toward serenity.

We have already talked about the need to let go of our childhood assumptions about God if they are not helping us to live with wisdom. We have talked about the need to accept ourselves and our social conditioning, which in turn can help us to accept other people. Letting go also helps in listening for divine guidance, for if we are clinging to our picture of what we assume we should be doing, we may not be open to noticing guidance that contradicts that picture. We may keep knocking on a door that God has closed, instead of noticing the open window.

Some people let go of their own volition, as Hilary Beard let go of her fear of economic insecurity to pursue her dream of writing, and Will Brock let go of his fear of his inner-city students. Many people, however, don't let go willingly. Dan Gottlieb made a point of saying that he was *forced* to learn to let go. Many others in this book had lessons thrust upon them that they would not have chosen for themselves. Sally Jergesen learned to let go when her husband walked out on her and their young son. Ro'Bin White Morton learned to let go sitting in the New Orleans Superdome after Hurricane Katrina. Celeste Zappala let go of hate after her son Sherwood was killed in Iraq. In none of these cases was letting go fun or easy. In most of these stories it was a process that took years.

My own lessons in acceptance have not been so dramatic. Often it's been the little things I've been challenged to let go of—a good night's sleep when a baby won't settle or time to write when an older relative needs to be brought to the hospital. Motherhood has been a continual training ground. When a child gets pinkeye, a fever, or (God forbid) head lice and can't go to school, my husband and I suddenly have to adjust work schedules to accommodate the surprise. As the person with the more flexible schedule, I'm usually the one to change my plans. Sometimes I'm grumpy about this, and sometimes I'm serene. The day goes better for everyone if I'm serene. There are also bigger surprises, such as a sudden trip to the emergency room after a bike accident, and mundane inconveniences, like a child leaving something white and sticky in a pocket so it gets smeared through an entire load of wash. They're teaching me to let go, these little angels of mine, which is good because I still need the practice.

We are all given practice, but some people never learn the lesson. I know an eighty-five-year-old woman who complains about her life every time you say hello to her. She complains that her children never visit her, and then when they do, she complains about everything they did wrong during the visit. "My son brought me a green pepper that cost four dollars," she told me recently, her eyes narrowing in disapproval at his extravagance.

"I could have killed him." And then she complained some more that he doesn't visit her enough, oblivious to the fact that her complaints might be driving him away. As Dan Gottlieb said of his friend who had the picture of the perfect man, this woman has a picture of perfect, frugal, and attentive children. Because she can't let go of her picture, she can't appreciate the children she does have. She also has a picture of herself as young and healthy and, like many people, is having a hard time letting go of that. She complains about standing for three hours as a bingo caller, even though most people her age would be grateful to have that stamina and social network. She is causing her own unhappiness by refusing to accept the things she cannot change, and it is sad to watch.

Park Dong-Sun cautions that we cannot learn to let go all of a sudden. "We move progressively, one step after another." He compares it to doing the Twelve Steps in AA or living out the lines of the Serenity Prayer. "There is no beginning, and no end." It is like a circle. He says that when he hears people in AA say, "Let go and let God," he translates it as the Buddhist teaching, "Let go of all your concepts of life." He notes most Buddhists are not able to truly practice this, though it is a powerful teaching. "Ultimately the Zen training and practice is to stop conceptualizing," he explains. "As soon as we conceptualize, we limit ourselves, and with that limitation, we cannot see the whole."

A recent experience with pneumonia reminded Fatima bin Mustafa to let go and trust that God could see the whole better than she could. A single mother who struggles to make ends meet, Fatima had found a promising new job and had gone through the training program. "In my mind, that was the solution to everything," she recalls. "Then I got sick, and I was so frustrated. I had no choice but to stop." Fatima was exhausted and worried about her messy house, but resisted sending her two children to her mother because she thought the children would be bored. "I had all these restrictions and boundaries, but Allah showed me, 'You have to send them to your mom. You're sick. Everything is going to be all right, so don't worry about that.' " When Fatima finally had to go to the hospital at three in the morning, a friend gave her a ride and took her children to their grandmother's, who happened to be off from work for a few days. "Within that horrific time for me, it still worked out. My children were taken care of, which is what I worried about the most." The job she got after her recovery is more flexible than the first one would have been, and that has been another blessing. "Allah knows best," Fatima says, explaining that the experience has helped her to stop thinking, " 'What if?' Because I had the what if, and it all worked out."

Like Dan and Dong-Sun, Fatima notes that learning to let go is a process that doesn't happen overnight, but step by step, like in school where you pass one grade and then move on to the next level. "If you claim to have faith, you will be tested," she says, recalling another recent incident when she hit a pothole and got a flat tire. As she sat with her children in the cold garage, her mechanic told her she would need a new rim, which she could barely afford. Then on closer inspection he realized the car frame was cracked and would cost $600 to $800 to fix. "I started crying hysterically," recalls Fatima, who couldn't imagine how she could balance her responsibilities without a car. Another woman in the waiting room heard Fatima crying and went out to her car for some money. Fatima tried to refuse, but the woman said, "Don't block my blessings, please," and tucked something into Fatima's pocket. "It was a hundred-dollar bill," she exclaims. "A stranger!" Two weeks later the mechanic found Fatima a good car at a bargain price. "Those are the types of things that happen just when you think, 'I can't do it anymore.' Allah shows you. So in the next go-round your faith is supposed to increase somewhat, and it does. When you think you're at that limit, you think back to the last time, and you strengthen yourself. You go forward, even if it's a baby step forward."

As Fatima notes, sometimes we move forward in baby steps. We unclench our hands a little bit each go-round. We can't *make* ourselves let go if we are not ready, and if we make serenity our new picture, we'll just get frustrated with ourselves every time we get frustrated, which is unlikely to help anything. We needn't feel bad about it if we don't face every $600 car repair cheerfully. What we can do is try to see each setback or inconvenience as an opportunity to develop wisdom. We can acknowledge our emotions, practice mindfulness and gratitude, and seek divine guidance. Instead of judging ourselves when we don't do these things perfectly, we can just remember that clinging to our thoughts about how we think things should be is unlikely to help us deal with how they are.

Although we can't make ourselves let go, there are things we can do to help ourselves. Dan mentioned practicing mindfulness, something we can do anytime, but which is facilitated by regular meditation. In chapter 2, Marcelle Martin mentioned going on retreat, which helped her let go of her fear of losing the relationship where she was silencing her heart. I have often found journal writing helpful in discharging my negative thoughts and emotions so something new can get in. On a few occasions, when I knew I really needed to let go of something big, I've gone on retreat, written all my fears in my journal, and then concocted some little letting-go ritual to help my heart make the shift. I've heard of others creating similar rituals, such as a young woman who went on a women's retreat and burned her wedding dress in the "letting go" campfire. Of course, you don't have to be quite that dramatic. Each person has to find the outward practices that will make an inward shift most likely.

LETTING GO

Identify something you have been carrying for too long, and designate a special time to act out your desire to let go of it. It could be a fear, a desire, a relationship, or something more concrete. Pick a special place where you won't be disturbed, perhaps somewhere outdoors where you can feel the earth and see the sky. Bring a journal and write, stream of consciousness style, about why you have been holding on to this thing and how it has become a burden to you. If relevant, write about how this burden is affecting other people. Name the fears that have prevented you from letting go before now, and imagine how good it would feel to be free of those fears. Then, on a separate piece of paper, draw or write a symbol of whatever you wish to let go of. It can be a word, a graphic picture, or whatever feels meaningful to you. Alternatively, you may wish to bring something from home that feels symbolic and that you are willing to destroy.

How you get rid of your symbol will depend on your circumstances. I am partial to a small fire in a fire pit, but if you live in a dry, fire-prone region, you might want to come up with something involving water, such as writing on biodegradable paper and tossing it into a stream or river. The main point is to find a symbolic way to demonstrate your desire to let go. Clasping your hands together and then releasing them to the sky might work just as well as a burning ritual, as might going to a church with intention candles and lighting one to symbolize your prayer of letting go. You have to find the act that feels appropriate to you.

Know that a letting-go ritual may bring an immediate feeling of release, or it may not. For many people, letting go is a slow journey, and this may be just one step.

Just as it helps to be gentle with ourselves, we must also beware of judging others or lecturing them on the benefits of letting go. I remember a friend who was having difficulty conceiving saying how frustrated she was that people kept telling her to let go of her deepest desire. They told her stories about women who got pregnant as soon as they had adopted, as if giving up guaranteed conception. My friend felt these stories cruelly made light of her hope and fueled it at the same time. Even so, I made this mistake not long ago with a different friend who was struggling to get pregnant. I was midway through a little speech on letting go and relaxing when I realized how it was hurting the friend I was trying to help. As Dan Gottlieb advised in chapter 5, loving someone and listening to them is more likely to help them than giving advice.

The stories about women getting pregnant after giving up are not totally apocryphal. There is evidence that in some cases women are more likely to get pregnant after they stop trying so hard, just as there is evidence that giving birth goes better when the mother is relaxed. Peter Warrington, the obstetrician from chapter 5, says that regardless of whether or not there is a supernatural explanation, there is a biological one. Stress can impact fertility, which is why many doctors tell women to take a vacation if they are trying unsuccessfully to get pregnant, "especially when there is no discernible medical reason," clarifies Peter. Likewise during labor he notes, "There's good evidence to show that just the degree of anxiety in and of itself, through a bunch of hormonal responses, interferes with labor and makes contractions less effective or less frequent." He concurs with Grace Potts, who in chapter 1 noted that teenagers sometimes have easier labors than older, more educated women, who are more prone to try to figure out and control the process.

Anxiety itself can have all kinds of negative effects. It affects not only your fertility but also your ability to fight infection and heal from illness. If you're a figure skater, it can impact your ability to land that triple axel in competition. (Ever notice how it is the skaters who look scared *before* the jump who usually fall?) Anxiety also limits your ability to see that of God in others or to listen deeply to them. In short, excessive anxiety can mess up all kinds of things. So, when your fear is the root of the problem you are facing, or even a major contributing factor, letting go can actually make what you are grasping for more likely to come to you. But here's the problem: fear isn't always the root cause, so letting go doesn't always bring a miraculous solution. Grace didn't just have anxiety; she had blocked fallopian tubes, which going on vacation would not have cured. Dan Gottlieb had a broken spine. He did eventually relinquish all hope of regaining feeling in his legs, but that did not lead to a miraculous recovery. Instead he expanded the feeling in his heart. Sally Jergesen let go of her desire to control her ex-husband, but that didn't make him come back. Sometimes letting go is described like it is some New Age trick for getting what you want, when in fact there are plenty of problems that letting go won't solve.

Even when letting go can't change the physical circumstances, however, it can still change the situation by changing your perspective on it. For Dan and Sally, letting go didn't mean getting back what they had lost; it meant getting on with their lives and finding other ways to be happy. When they stopped grasping, they felt better. My friend who was frustrated by all the people who told her she might get pregnant if she let go did eventually relinquish her hope of getting pregnant. The fruit wasn't an unexpected pregnancy, but the adoption of two wonderful children. She got what she most wanted, to be a mother, but not in the way she had initially pictured. If she had continued clinging to her dream of a biological child, she might have missed out on the blessings she did receive.

Still, there is something mysterious about this letting-go stuff that goes beyond stress hormones and logical explanations. It relates to the Taoist idea of *wu wei* or the Baptist preacher's advice about swimming in the direction of the current. It relates to way opening when we get out of the way. In other words, it has a spiritual dimension. It's not just that we are relaxing our efforts; we are making room for something else. "Let go and let God," says the old adage. While some, like Dong-Sun, would see letting go as a valuable practice regardless of whether or not you believe in God, for those who do have faith in a Higher Power, part of the comfort comes from trusting that there is a bigger plan that we can't see. Fatima, for example, thought of letting go not as giving up, but as accepting God's greater perspective on what she needed. This faith can bring people comfort in all kinds of circumstances.

Letting go is not the same as quitting something forever, as Timothy Olsen learned while training as a sculptor. "One of my professors would always say, 'When you're having a problem with your work and you can't make up your mind how to do something, go and make yourself a cup of tea.' At the time I thought, 'Oh, I should go to the cafeteria, have a coffee, a beer, a glass of wine, or whatever and leave the problem back at the studio.' Over time I've come to understand that he wasn't saying that. He was saying, 'Make yourself a cup of tea.' " Timothy explains that drawing the water, bringing it to a boil, heating the teapot or the cup, infusing the tea, and then waiting, experiencing the odors, and drinking it is much more meditative than going to the café and having a coffee or a beer. "He was encouraging me to take the time to do something else and let the Spirit guide me through the quiet meditation of thinking of other things." Today Timothy notes that for many of his sculpture students, tapping away on the stones can provide the same release from their usual thoughts and worries.

Melvin Metelits recalls that when he was being treated for throat cancer, his radiologist often asked him what he was doing in his life, outside his cancer treatments. When Melvin told him that he was trying to relearn classical guitar, the doctor said, "Very good. That can be better than radiation." What he meant, Melvin explains, is that playing the guitar was meditative and relaxing and, as a result, deeply healing. Melvin agreed. As he said in chapter 3, "I had to have the serenity to know that I could not change what was, and the courage to proceed with the best treatment available to me." Learning to let go of the anxiety that had plagued him in his youth may have contributed to his physical healing, but it definitely helped to heal his spirit.

In *Spontaneous Healing: How to Discover and Enhance Your Body's Natural Ability to Maintain and Heal Itself*, Dr. Andrew Weil notes that modern Western medicine often uses violent imagery to describe its response to disease. We talk about the "war on cancer" and the "arsenal" of available drugs. Patients often exclaim, "I'm going to fight this thing!" in response to a life-threatening illness. Weil observes, "Over the years that I have been interviewing men and women who have experienced healing, I have come to feel that 'fighting this thing' may not be the best way to obtain the desired result." Rather, Weil argues, accepting the circumstances of one's life, including one's illness, appears to promote healing. "This change allows profound internal relaxation, so that people need no longer feel compelled to maintain a defensive stance toward life. Often, it occurs as part of a spiritual awakening and submission to a higher power." Weil notes that such total acceptance is "the most common correlation I observe between mind and healing in people with chronic illness."

Andrew Weil does not equate acceptance with doing nothing, refusing treatment in the name of faith. He advocates many tools that can promote health and healing, from eating more garlic and less white bread to undergoing major surgery. In fact, he points out that the patients who are most persistent and ask the most questions about their care are often the ones with the best results. This apparent paradox is confirmed by Susan Silberstein, founder of the Center for Advancement in Cancer Education. Dr. Silberstein describes one of the common traits of those who experience remarkable recoveries: "They accept the diagnosis but reject the prognosis." In other words, they practice serenity and courage at the same time, accepting the reality of their disease while doing what they can to make themselves well.

Accepting "That Death Thing"

When I interviewed Sophie Williamson, she had been diagnosed with chronic lymphocytic leukemia four years earlier and was experiencing complications from polymyalgia rheumatica, an autoimmune disease. Close to seventy, she believed she was dying, which is why I interviewed her while the idea for this book was still germinating, years before I conducted most of the other interviews. It's for this reason that we have a little more hindsight on Sophie's experience.

As Sophie explained in previous chapters, she had a strong "fix it" impulse for most of her life, but dealing with cancer helped her learn to let go and trust her inner guidance. A few weeks after her diagnosis, Sophie dreamed of a great sleeping bear between her breasts. A friend schooled in alternative health methods encouraged her to do directed visualizations with the bear, explaining that some cancer patients visualize things like little machine guns destroying their cancer. Sophie couldn't relate to such violent imagery, but she did direct the bear to lick up her cancer cells. "I started telling the bear what to do," she recalls with regret. "Instead of saying, 'What lessons do you have for me?' I put him to work."

After weeks of trying the visualizations, Sophie realized this approach wasn't working. "So I started to ask the bear questions, and the bear said, 'We don't know enough about this disease.' " The bear—which Sophie believes to be the part of her that is connected to a higher spiritual source of power and knowledge that we can all access—gave her two technical medical questions for her oncologist, questions that Sophie herself would not have known enough to ask. Her doctor patiently answered, explaining how the now cancerous cells had been produced originally by her thymus, which is located between the breasts. "Good call," said the doctor when she told him that was where the bear appeared.

Sophie didn't want to do war with her body, so she decided to try to improve her health with good food, exercise, and some medication, but not chemotherapy—a decision that she notes would not be right for everyone, but that came from her own inner guidance. "I have no need to control," she explains in her high soft voice, "except I want to make the decisions about treatment. I don't want to turn it over to the doctors and have them trying to control everything." She developed a strong relationship with her oncologist, but told him, "Look, I respect your knowledge, and I need it, but I'm going to do this differently maybe than you. I am just really comfortable now with this. I believe that I have healing powers inside of myself, and I will heal whatever I need to heal." Acknowledging that her healing might be emotional or spiritual rather than physical, she added, "That doesn't mean I'm going to get well." Four years into the disease Sophie said she was at complete peace with her cancer. "It's just as much a part of me as the color of my skin or my eyes now." The irony is that after her total acceptance, Sophie had a spontaneous remission, something her doctor said never happened with her kind of cancer. She died six years after our interview of a heart attack, totally cancer free.

In many ways, Sophie exemplifies the message of the Serenity Prayer. Although she accepted her diagnosis with remarkable serenity, she knew that her choices did matter. She had initially hoped for a spontaneous remission, which is why she tried the visualization technique with the bear. Even when she was told that remissions never happened with her kind of cancer, she wanted to stay healthy for as long as possible, for the sake of her daughters as much as herself. To these ends, she asked for extra time to talk to her doctor, requested pictures of her cancer cells so she could visualize them, and asked questions that came from a bear. She was not necessarily an easy patient. But while she was involved with every decision regarding her care, she wasn't attached to a particular outcome. She described her journey as "entering a stream" and just going along with the flow. She practiced *wu wei*, and the result was a better medical outcome than doctors would have predicted with the most aggressive chemotherapy, though Sophie would have been the first to say that her approach was not designed to trick death. Her acceptance was genuine.

Many of us yearn for the kind of peace Sophie felt about her life. We wish we could face the evening commute with the same equanimity she felt in facing her diagnosis. We wish we could make peace with our pasts without having to contract a disease. We wish we could live focused lives that help others. But we don't necessarily want to do one of the key things Sophie did. We don't want to accept our own mortality.

At first, accepting the inevitability of death may seem very different from the other lessons in this book, such as accepting ourselves and our inner guidance. However, *The Tibetan Book of Living and Dying* asserts that "the deepest reason why we are afraid of death is [that] we do not know who we are." The author explains that if we have built our lives on the fragile ground of social status or convention we will be especially afraid to let go in the end. This may well be true. It seems that often the people who are most anxious about their lives are also most anxious about their deaths. On the other hand, if we have a strong sense of who we are and what our purpose here is, we may better be able to recognize when that purpose is fulfilled. Letting go of our fear of life's end can be a crucial step in finding serenity.

"In Tibetan the word for body is *lü*, which means 'something you leave behind,' like baggage," explains *The Tibetan Book of Living and Dying*. "Each time we say '*lü*,' it reminds us that we are only travelers, taking temporary refuge in this life and this body." Accepting the reality of death, author Sogyal Rinpoche explains, deeply affects how we live. When we have a true awareness of life's impermanence, we don't put our energy into acquiring or protecting material possessions. We act out of compassion, rather than fear. Rinpoche notes that when he first came to the West, he was shocked by the way most people lived either in denial of death or in terror of it: "The longer we postpone facing death, the more we ignore it, the greater the fear and insecurity that build up to haunt us. The more we try to run away from that fear, the more monstrous it becomes." In other words, we'll never experience serenity until we accept the inevitability of death.

This idea is not unique to Buddhism. In fact, it runs through all spiritual traditions in one form or another. "The prophet Mohammed said that a strong believer is more useful than a weak believer," explains Malik Mubashshir. "So exercise, fitness, new technology in terms of life extension, these are all good—as long as you don't lose the perspective that you will die. There is no indefinite life. You will face death. In fact there is a segment of Islamic opinion that really focuses on death a great deal. I guess it is similar to some of the medieval Catholic reflections on death," he notes, pointing out that the prophet said things like, "Don't assume when you see the morning that you will live to see the evening," or "Don't assume in the evening that you will live to see the morning." Imam Malik acknowledges that he used to find this constant reiteration of death very disturbing, but as he gets older it seems less strange. "Death is all around. If you don't have some kind of philosophical framework to deal with that, it would just be completely overwhelming."

What does it mean to accept death in practical terms, especially when we are facing illness? Religious people have come up with a mind-boggling range of answers. Members of the Faith Tabernacle church believe that sickness is caused by the devil, and only God can heal. For this reason, Dennis and Lorie Nixon refused to seek medical treatment for their children, allowing two of them to die from medical conditions that prosecutors deemed treatable. Even though the deaths earned the Nixons jail time away from their ten other children, they were unrepentant. In a *60 Minutes* interview with the family, interviewer Ed Bradley asked the couple, "Does man have any role in healing?" The Nixons answered a resounding, "No."

Most religious people across traditions would not agree with the Nixons, including Sophie Williamson, who only refused chemotherapy because it was what her inner guidance told her to do. Although we must ultimately accept death, that does not mean we must passively accept every infection, snubbing antibiotics and refusing to change what we could change with little risk or effort. Most people agree that healing is an appropriate use of human powers. The expansion of medical technology is blurring the line between what we should and shouldn't control, however. In the United States more than $90 billion is spent per year just on end-of-life care, although those treatments are often unsuccessful, invasive, and more than the patient wanted. When are our attempts to prolong life a way of honoring life's sacredness, and when are they futile attempts to deny death? There is no simple answer, but it is important to recognize that in many cases our medical system bends too far in the direction of trying to deny death, partly because of fear of liability, but also because patients and their families are afraid to let go.

Sophie was unusual in her attitude toward death. Most of us fear the end of this life, even if we do believe in an afterlife. We even fear to talk about it, as if acknowledging death will be the crack in the door that lets in the Grim Reaper. My husband,

Tom, a hospice social worker, observes that often adult children lie to their aging parents about their prognosis, though usually the dying parents confess to Tom that they know what is really going on. In fact, something similar happened to Sophie at the beginning of her illness. Her physician daughter had ordered extra tests when Sophie's white cell count was unusually high, but didn't explain why, simply telling Sophie she had a blood disorder and needed to see a specialist. It wasn't until Sophie read "Oncologist" on the office door that she realized why she had been so tired. Once she understood, she said she appreciated that her daughter was trying to protect her by carrying the burden for her, but, "I don't want any of my daughters to carry me like that."

Trying to shield our loved ones from death only keeps them from accessing their own wisdom about what they need. It also shields them from the clarity that dying can bring. Sophie said of her own illness, "I never understood before when I heard people say that these kinds of things can be gifts, but it really is a gift." One part of the gift was becoming clear that her work involved helping children and feeling empowered to say "no" to everything else. If she had never been told what was wrong with her, she would have missed this opportunity to become clear about her purpose. She would have picked up on the unexplained anxiety of her daughters, without having the chance to come to peace herself.

The fact that my mother was comfortable talking about death made her final year, and the period after her death, much easier for me. On the practical side, she told me where her safe-deposit key was and what was in the box. She told me where she wanted her funeral and even what saint she wanted on her prayer cards. During her last week of life, she had me read through her entire address book as she told me exactly whom to call when she died, pointing out who had gone before her so I wouldn't waste my time on disconnected numbers. Her practicality was a great gift. In contrast, when her brother died a few years before, he refused to tell anyone where his safe-deposit key was hidden, not wanting to admit that a time would come when he wouldn't be there.

Of course, accepting death is difficult for most people. Even though my mother kept saying she was ready to die, making jokes about death up until the end, there was still some part of her that kept fighting for control. She never felt Sophie's serenity. Instead she kept asking the hospice nurse to tell her exactly how much time she had left, as if she could schedule her departure. Even at sixty pounds, she insisted on making her own breakfast and going to the bathroom alone. At one point the hospice social worker observed, "You must have been fighting hard to live." My mother nodded and said, "I wanted to die young, but there must be some subconscious part of me that wants to fight."

That ferocious will to live was one of my mother's strengths. As a baby, she had the measles and was the only child on the hospital ward at the time to survive the disease. If one of my children gets that sick, I will hope they inherited their grandmother's tenacity. But at the end of her life, my mother's drive became a burden more than a gift. She fought her helplessness, making her care more difficult for both of us. I remember her laboring to lift a spoonful of ice cream to her mouth, missing by a few inches and then muttering in disgust. She just hated being fed, even though I was there and willing to feed her.

Although I admired the way she spoke openly about her death, I was sad that she wasn't able to let go and accept help during the final hours of her life. Because she couldn't accept her powerlessness, she suffered more than she needed to.

Like many people, watching her parents age is forcing Tracey Smith-Diggs to think about her own mortality, though her wording reflects the awkwardness of the subject. "I want to get to the point of being able to let go, if something ever happens to me—that death thing—realizing that it could happen at any time, but just being thankful for the life that I have. There's probably more fear of how I'm going to die than the actual death," she says quietly, acknowledging how frightened she is of becoming helpless or dependent. She reminisces about her aunt who just died in her eighties, even though she had cancer when she was young. "She really lived life," concludes Tracey. "She didn't let any grass grow under her feet. That's how I want to be. I want to live my life." David Watt has also been trying to get more comfortable with his mortality, especially since his father's death. A college professor with a wry sense of humor, David reminds himself, "Thus far most people who have been born have died, and if present trends continue, that might happen to me, too." Although he is making fun of himself with the abstract wording, he is actually acknowledging death more clearly than many people do before they land in the emergency room or the oncologist's office and are faced with a battery of tests and decisions along with the need to acknowledge their mortality.

End-of-life decisions are an area where listening to our inner guidance can be particularly important. This is the advice given by Warren Ostrom, a Quaker who has been a geriatric social worker for more than twenty years. Ostrom notes that often patients and their families do whatever doctors tell them will keep them alive longest. As a result, he has heard many patients complain that they've lived "too long," and has seen too many families spend their last dollar on medical treatment that could have saved many more lives if invested in prenatal care. A man of deep faith, he argues, "Death is nothing to resist," though he also acknowledges that there are times when prolonging life is probably the right thing to do. Instead of giving a clear-cut set of guidelines, he suggests prayerfully listening to God's guidance about when to pursue life-prolonging treatment. He suggests clearness committees and queries. One of the questions he raises is "whether you have unfinished work, or if you are free to go." It sounds like a straightforward question, but we won't be able to answer it unless we know who we are and what our purpose has been.

Asking whether we are free to go may force us to acknowledge all we have not accomplished in life. We may have to let go of our youthful, ambitious pictures of ourselves. At fifty-two, Jorge Arauz admits with a laugh, "I grew up with expectations about myself that were uncommon, but I find myself being a very common human being." Jorge is a professional counselor who also facilitates Alternatives to Violence workshops in the United States, as well as in his native Ecuador and other Latin American countries. He intentionally moved to a violent urban neighborhood, but his original hope of founding a group house that would be a peaceful presence in the neighborhood has not been fully realized. Although his peace work is respected by those who know him, when Jorge thinks about his mortality, he feels he hasn't done much worth remembering. He acknowledges struggling to accept himself and other people. Of the fact that he won't change the world as much as he had hoped, he says, "This has been another thing to accept."

Imam Malik, who is approaching middle age himself, is also grappling with the limits of his own accomplishments, especially in terms of his impact on the world. "I was feeling really low a few months ago," he recalls. "I talked to someone I've known a long time, who is also a devout Muslim, and we realized we were going through a similar awakening, although it didn't feel like an awakening at the time." She said, 'When you're growing up, you know you are going to transform the world. You'll eliminate racism in your lifetime. You'll eliminate sexism in your lifetime. And at some point you look and go, 'Wow, this is still going to be here when I'm gone. Damn. I could live, and I could die, and the world would not have transformed in the way that I had hoped.'"

Malik laughs, saying that the woman's comments jolted him with their truth. "It seems naïve and funny to say it," he admits, though that reality has been sinking into him. Malik has long worked against injustice and acknowledges that much has changed in his lifetime—especially in terms of racism and sexism. But he notes, "Ultimately it's not really mine to solve. I play my role, strut my hour on the stage, and then I'm gone. The idea is to try to do as much as I can, to the best of my ability, in community with other people of like mind, transform as much as we can, but this is not paradise, and it's not likely to be paradise anytime soon. Psychologically, this is where spiritual trust in a benevolent creator who has a plan is comforting. But it's not a placebo. It's not a cure-all because so much responsibility is on us." In other words, we shouldn't ignore the problems of the world, but we must let go of our ambitions to solve them all ourselves.

DEALING WITH THE UNACCEPTABLE

As noted in chapter 1, sometimes the spiritual ideal of acceptance has been misused to keep people quiet about things that are unfair. They've been told that their poverty or lack of power must be "God's will," so don't complain. The ideal of forgiveness has been twisted to mean: don't criticize the unjust, don't question what is wrong. Martin Luther King, Jr., for example, was criticized by Southern, white preachers for opposing segregation, though as King pointed out, those same preachers never raised their voices against Jim Crow. While there are plenty of examples of this in history, it's not necessarily only a problem of the past. bell hooks, a black Buddhist and well-known author (who writes her pen name in lowercase letters), says that when black Buddhists speak overtly against domination in Buddhist circles, they "are often seen as not spiritual enough." Let go, they are told. The problem is not discrimination, but your idealism—your picture of how things should be.

I appreciate the Dalai Lama's response to this dilemma. In *Mindful Politics: A Buddhist Guide to Making the World a Better Place,* he writes, "Of the many problems we face today, some are natural calamities, which must be accepted and faced with equanimity. Others, however, are of our own making, created by misunderstanding, and can be corrected." They, of course, are the things that should be changed. We will prolong our own suffering if we don't let go of our striving and our anger, but that doesn't mean we should be silent or complacent. In fact, not doing anything in the face of human suffering may signal a lack of compassion or laziness, rather than spiritual maturity.

How to accept other people without condoning the unfair things they sometimes do is one of the trickiest aspects of the wisdom to know the difference. "That racism thing still has me stumped," says Yvonne Thompson, whose six-year-old grandson came home one day after being called a "nigger" at his predominantly white school. "That's not a nice thing to call someone, is it?" he asked Yvonne, who had raised him since he was a baby. "What do you say to a child?" she asks. She shakes her head, still baffled by what causes such hate. She called the principal, who brought in the white boy's parents so Yvonne could meet with them. "What can I do to help you to see me as a person?" she asked them, though they didn't have an answer. "They were horribly embarrassed, and I was angry," she recalls.

Reflecting on it in hindsight, Yvonne notes that when you see something wrong, "you have to speak up about it," though that doesn't mean you should get stuck in anger. As she's gotten older she has come to realize that she can't change other people. "You cannot make Mrs. Green who is white live next door to me," she says. "You can't make her because she can move." When Yvonne moved to her middle-class neighborhood decades ago, it was eighty percent white, with many retired judges and schoolteachers. "But then white flight hit," notes Yvonne. "I had to learn that I couldn't make these people stay here if that's not what they wanted to do." She says she does have a responsibility to be the best neighbor she can be and to speak up when she sees something wrong, but that doesn't mean she can control anyone else.

It is one thing to accept that you can't make someone fall in love with you or make your parents age the way you think they should, but accepting that you can't change things that you think are downright wrong can be particularly difficult, especially if you are prone to idealism, as I am.

"There's a lot of tension between utopian desires and what really happens," says David Watt, who notes that the university where he teaches is very hierarchical. "It's not so difficult with people below you on the hierarchy. You can just go out of your way to treat them respectfully," he explains. "With people above you on the hierarchy, it's more challenging. Occasionally I just dig in my heels, probably in a not very Christian way, with an attitude of 'You're trying to bully me or someone else, and you're not going to get away with it.' " As the new director of graduate studies, David has to deal with many problems that he considers "annoying," so he reminds himself that he asked for the job. "That's what it means to be director of graduate studies," he tells himself. "People will come to you with really annoying problems. Now that you notice it's annoying, go on."

David finds humor is often more effective than self-righteousness, making fun of himself as well as others. He gives the example of a recent cocktail party where a colleague said, "I don't like to brag, but there's a new alumni magazine for Harvard University, and I was named one of the hundred most important alumni of all time." David, himself a Harvard grad, responded, "That's so funny. I was a hundred and one." He laughs loudly. "Humor does deflate, but it doesn't make for a revolution."

Although he is critical of the injustices of our society, David does not believe that every person is called to start a revolution. As he said in chapter 3, he believes that "a lot of one's job is just to stay in one's own lane." He says it is arrogant to think we can solve all the world's problems, and feeling responsible for too much can be a way of not doing anything.

Dan Gottlieb is clear about where his lane is. Although all the proceeds of his books go to charity, and he sometimes attends political rallies, his primary way of making a difference is as a therapist. "I think about the world, and I'm not thrilled with many aspects of it. I'm not thrilled that my grandson is going to grow up in this world. So the question is, between now and the time I have left, what do I want to do about it? I don't want to put bullets in a gun. And I don't want to clench my fist and beat up on institutions that cause pain, even though that might be a very right thing to do. My take is that the world is alienated and isolated and lacking in compassion and humanity. It's lacking in love and simple care, and therefore it's my responsibility to teach that, to do that, to be that. To add more of that to the world because I believe it's contagious. So rather than fight against injustice, as a therapist, my wish is to heal the pain and ignorance and fear that caused it in the first place." For example, if treating someone who is stuck in an abusive marriage, Dan focuses on the patient's insecurity, rather than on the abuse. "If you are in an abusive marriage, it's because you're insecure, 'cause you don't think you'll be okay outside of the marriage. So what needs to be addressed is your own fear and your own insecurity. If you can learn to live with your own insecurity and accept it, then you're not stuck in the marriage anymore."

Several of the stories in this book have included people getting unstuck from abusive situations. They couldn't change the perpetrators, but they could accept the reality of the situation and then leave. Because of the same strong self-respect that they passed on to their daughter, Joan Countryman's parents left the Deep South before the civil rights era, rather than accept Jim Crow laws. Ro'Bin White Morton left a violent marriage rather than accept abuse after God's voice gave her the courage to do so. Tracey Smith-Diggs left a university job where the people she reported to were not abusive but very negative. Tracey's fear of financial insecurity prompted her to go back a few months later, despite what she felt was the guidance of the Holy Spirit, until getting fired confirmed that her original impulse had been correct. Tracey's experience reminds us that sometimes accepting the truth of a situation and facing our own insecurity is harder than putting up with something we know isn't right.

There is a stereotype of letting go, an image of sanguine passivity that is not accurate. Sometimes letting go is actively courageous. Especially if you see something unacceptable and don't have the power to change it, letting go may mean being willing to walk away. Like the Jews who followed Moses across the sea or Abraham in the story Dan cited, you might even have to leave everything that is familiar.

A Jewish woman, born in Yugoslavia in the 1930s, Dr. Eva Ray recalls her father's decision to get his family out of Europe after reading Adolf Hitler's *Mein Kampf* in the 1920s. It took years to get a visa to the United States, where he hoped to bring his wife and two daughters after he was settled, though tragically he died of appendicitis en route to the United States. Eva's mother immediately put their names on a list to take her husband's place, against the wishes of her mother and five siblings, who all said, "You're crazy to leave." When the Germans invaded Yugoslavia in 1941, getting out became even more difficult, but Eva's mother persisted. "She sat in that consulate office every day after the Germans came, waiting for the U.S. visa," recalls Eva. "Our number came up just as the Germans took over the American consulate office. The next day, with the Americans gone, we couldn't have left." A few years later Eva's mother received a telegram informing her that the beloved family she had left behind was all dead.

While Eva's mother exhibited the courage to change what she could change for herself and her two daughters, she also demonstrated the ability to accept adversity calmly. Even with a visa, their journey out of Europe took years and brought them through Berlin during the British bombing. "Everything was bombed around us, and we were in the cellars every night," recalls Eva, who was eight at the time. Her mother would whisper in German, "The English are bombing, so we should be very grateful. It's good, but *shh*." Eva laughs that her mother was so optimistic, despite the terrifying circumstances. "My mother always picked out the good in every situation," says Eva, who believes her mother's attitude and optimism helped Eva weather the traumas of her childhood and become an optimistic person herself.

Being able to accept terrible circumstances need not make us passive, as Eva's mother shows. Although she was not religious and wouldn't have described her inner guidance as divinely inspired, she had a strong inner sense of what she should do and was brave enough to follow it, even when those she loved thought she was foolish. She knew she couldn't change the Nazis, but she could get her daughters out of their way.

There are times when getting out of the way and keeping a positive attitude are the best we can do. There are also times when, as the Dalai Lama said, we need to stand and solve the problems that are solvable, instead of running away from them. Whether this is possible often depends on whether or not we are alone. While it is certainly understandable that Joan Countryman's parents felt the need to get out of the Deep South to escape Jim Crow, it's useful to remember that only a few years later ordinary people like them banded together and were able to overturn the laws that drove the Countrymans away.

Often, in dealing with social problems, what we need to let go of is the assumption that we have to figure everything out ourselves. In fact, we cannot truly understand "our lane," to use David Watt's football analogy, without viewing ourselves as part of the team of community, as we'll see in the next chapter.

Queries

What "pictures" of your life do you carry?

What is your worst "what if"?

What are the experiences that have forced you to let go?

What do you still find difficult to accept?

Are there things that might get easier if you stopped trying so hard?

Are you able to speak openly about your own mortality?

How do you feel about your "unfinished business"?

What problems in the world do you consider "unacceptable," and how do you deal with them?

Seven

FINDING WISDOM
IN COMMUNITY

Timothy Olsen grew up Episcopalian, and as a teenager became the most actively religious person in his family. In college he questioned his faith and stopped going to church for a while, but creating art nurtured his "belief in things unseen" and his sense that he could feel God's guidance in his life. When he came back to the church in his twenties, it was partly because he felt called to be an ordained minister. "It developed out of a sense that I could help other people," he explains.

Timothy's sense of calling was confirmed as he became active in church programs and was affirmed for his work, especially with youth, and found joy in it. For years, he dodged the call, however, afraid that the church would not ordain him because he was gay. Eventually he mustered the courage to take some steps, beginning the diocese's three-year program for potential applicants to test whether they are really called to ministry before

EILEEN FLANAGAN

being accepted into the seminary. He also asked his congregation for a discernment group—a few people trained in deep, prayerful listening to support a person who is seeking God's guidance. "There were two main things that came out of the discernment group," Timothy recalls. "One was, 'You need to continue with the process as it's outlined,' and the other was, 'Be patient and trust God.' Those turned out to be very good words and words that I really didn't want to hear," he admits with a laugh. He was all right with taking the next steps in the application process, but being patient and trusting were not always easy.

By this time, the sexual abuse scandal in the Roman Catholic Church had broken out, and the Episcopal hierarchy was fearful of scandal in its own church, adding to Timothy's fear that he might be rejected because of his sexual orientation. Despite this worry, he experienced many affirmations that he was on the right path. "My discernment group, rector, spiritual adviser, and therapist all felt that my call was genuine, and I felt it was, too," says Timothy. When his local congregation decided to bless same-sex partnerships, he felt affirmed and hopeful. "Through the process I doubled or tripled the things that I was doing at the church," he recalls. "Perhaps it was wishful thinking, but I believed that because these activities worked out and seemed beneficial for others that this also was an affirmation." On a trip to a monastic community in France he felt more inward confirmation. "I felt clear," he recalls.

A year into the preparation process, Timothy met with the local bishop and was told that he could not be ordained: there was fear that because he was gay he might be perceived as a threat by the public. "They were focusing on other people's perceptions, whether they were based on reality or speculation, and that was really disturbing," recalls Timothy, who felt betrayed by the institutional church. Adding injury to insult, the same day as his conversation with the bishop, Timothy was a passenger in a car that was rear-ended, leading him to spend the next six months in doctors' offices. Ironically, the accident helped him to let go, forcing him to see it as a period for healing and restructuring his life. Through the restructuring, he held on to the much-repeated (literally!) quotation from the fourteenth-century mystic Julian of Norwich: "All shall be well; and all shall be well; and all manner of things shall be well." Despite the difficulty, it was true. "I felt God helping me in the healing process," he recalls, leading him to gradually let go of his anger and accept the bishop's decision, though he still disagrees with it.

Now, nearly seven years later, Timothy is a professional sculptor, who finds joy teaching sculpture and volunteering at his church. "The call to help and work with others is still there and still very strong, but really there are other ways to do it," he says, adding with a laugh, "I have a very strong dislike of the statement 'When God closes a door He opens a window,' and yet it's been my experience that that is true. Both the openings and closings are expressions of God's love. They can be painful, but we grow from the experiences."

One of the fruits of Timothy's painful rejection from ordained ministry was a new appreciation of community. "I received a lot of support from people that was very beneficial in the healing process," he recalls. "God was present in the people who sat with me, who cried with me, who tried to make me laugh in that period, and who encouraged me to stay involved." At first Timothy felt annoyed that people kept asking him to volunteer for different church projects, but he gradually came to realize that it was a way of affirming his gifts and that church was really about the people rather than the hierarchical structure. "The realization that church is about community, that in community we can support one another, help one another, and build each other up—those are simple realizations that everybody believes and knows. Why didn't I believe it, and why didn't I accept it?" He acknowledges that he did know the value of community intellectually. "Knowing it in the heart and soul is more real than knowing it upstairs," he observes.

FINDING GOD AND OURSELVES IN COMMUNITY

Timothy's story illustrates many of the themes in this book. He has gradually come to know himself and trust his inner guidance, but he has still had to deal with the prejudices of other people, some of which he has been unable to change. After finally finding the courage to pursue ordained ministry, he was forced to let go of that dream and accept a decision he believed was wrong. One of the things that helped Timothy most was having a supportive community. Community can soften the blows of disappointment or struggle, helping us find serenity. Sometimes community can also give us courage and the strength in numbers that enable us to change much more than any of us could accomplish alone. Finally, community helps us develop wisdom. It is sometimes through seeing that of God in other people, and having them reflect that of God in us, that we can sense how the Spirit is lead-ing us.

We have already heard many stories in this book of people who found serenity and courage in part by finding the right com-munity. When Hilary Beard discovered a more loving concept of God in a new church, it helped give her the courage to leave a soul-deadening job and follow her dream of becoming a full-time writer. Matthew Cole, Yvonne Thompson, and Park Dong-Sun all felt saved by the fellowship of Twelve Step programs and the example of other alcoholics who had become sober. Matthew shared how the honesty of people in AA as well as his faith com-munity helped him break through denial and see himself more clearly, while spiritual teacher Marcelle Martin observed that relationships with other people can be an intense spiritual prac-tice, if you see them that way. Many spiritual writers across a range of traditions have argued that community helps us to dis-cover both our True Selves and the Divine. This is not because community is always easy, but because the challenges of living with others can bring out the best (and worst) in us.

Spiritual community, or *sangha*, is considered an important part of Buddhist practice. Often the term refers to monastic com-munity, but it can also be applied more broadly. Park Dong-Sun explains that most people are motivated by selfishness, but that living with others tempers this impulse and forces people to fol-low what Buddhists call precepts, which are like commandments (i.e., do not kill; do not lie; do not commit adultery). He points out that these teachings are universal and that there are usually harsh consequences in the community for breaking them. "*Sangha* is like a nurse who administers medication," says Dong-Sun, who has experienced both Buddhist community and the fellowship of Alcoholics Anonymous. "The teaching—Twelve Step teaching, Buddhist teaching, or biblical teaching—is like the medicine. The Buddha, God, Jesus, or Christ is the doctor. The teaching is medicine, and the community is the nurse that administers it." Having been forced by the community to control our behavior, we can then work on controlling our minds.

Now in his late sixties, Dong-Sun notes that he no longer has to force himself to observe the precepts. "It's just natural. Today the thought of harming others doesn't occur to me because I have a better understanding of the meaning of life. If I hurt others, I am hurting myself, not just emotionally but physically. Suppose I hurt the farmers, in my community or throughout the world; humanity will starve to death. So I am killing myself. I don't know how to build a house. I don't know how to weave clothes. I don't know how to build automobiles. So I realize, hey, I don't know much." He pauses with an intent look and adds, "Nothing can exist by itself."

The Buddhist belief in the interconnectedness of all life is shared by wisdom traditions all over the world. Yvonne Thompson learned this truth gradually and now finds great comfort in it. "There is no separation. Whether it is in Darfur, or France, or Swaziland, or Georgia, if it affects him, it affects me." Realizing that she was connected to others helped in her recovery from depression and addiction. "Lots of people reached out to help me, you know. The more people reached out to help me, the more confidence I had in myself." Although Yvonne no longer suffers as she did in her youth, she notes, "There are still days when the world may not look as bright as it did yesterday." Instead of feeling helpless, she says, "I'll call a therapist, and we'll have a little chat. Or I'll call one of my Twelve Step buddies, and we'll have a chat. I used to believe I could live alone within myself, and now, of course, I know I can't. I really, really need people. I believe we all do, but I *know* I do."

We don't need other people just for what they can do for us, but also for the good drawn out of us when we do things for them. Matthew Cole explains that Bill Wilson, one of the founders of Alcoholics Anonymous, discovered that helping others was a necessary part of helping himself. Bill had been staying sober by turning his personal will over to a Higher Power, but he was disheartened that many of the other alcoholics he was trying to help were not doing as well. He feared his new program wasn't working until his wife pointed out that *he* wasn't drinking, and he was the one reaching out to others. Helping other alcoholics became an essential part of the Twelve Step Program. I recently heard a similar story about a wealthy businessman who had suffered from depression for years. In addition to therapeutic treatment, he has found that reaching out to other depressed businessmen and helping them face their condition is one of the best things he can do for his own mental health.

Feeling that what we do helps others can build our own courage, optimism, and resilience, thus helping us to see our own strengths. For Ro'Bin White Morton, finding ways to support other survivors of Hurricane Katrina has been empowering. Now living in the North with her husband, she notes that the social service agencies charged with helping displaced Katrina survivors were not able to meet all their needs, particularly replacing the warm New Orleans culture. Ro'Bin started organizing the survivors in her area to support one another and began an annual party for Katrina survivors, the Krewe of Ferdonia Mardi Gras Box Float Parade, inviting local schoolchildren and people from the surrounding community to eat red beans and rice and strut to live jazz. "I've been called to serve," she says. "I'm very passionate about it. What I love about my new home is that every single gift God has given to me I can share with someone here." She brings out a children's book she is writing about the storm and tells me about Michael White, the artist who has agreed to illustrate it. This has affirmed her sense that she is on the right path. "I can turn that whole experience of Hurricane Katrina into something new and exciting and share my craft," she explains. "I know God wants me here."

Just as working in community can empower people to improve their circumstances, it can also give people support and peace of mind in facing life's unavoidable difficulties. "My mother is living with me, and she's on hospice," explains Eileen Smith, who has no siblings or other family to help her as she cares for her mother while running the Face to Face program that provides food and services to poor people. Although Eileen is alone in the middle of the night when she checks to see if her mother is still breathing, she says she is lucky because she never feels alone. "I have these concentric circles of community holding me every day. It is so real to me. It is what holds me up these days as my mother is getting near the end. I will never think of this time without thinking of the experience of community, from the people next door who stop in and say, 'How are you?' to the parish community, the friends I have who stand with me, to the Sisters of Saint Joseph, and the hospice community. It is a wonderful blessing. I don't believe I could be doing this without community."

Many people have to make their own support systems deliberately, either by seeking out neighbors or a religious congregation or by gathering people themselves. When I lived in the Pennsylvania mountains for a few years, I was part of a small worship group of friends who shared a desire for spiritual community. Each Sunday we gathered in one person's home for forty-five minutes of silent worship, followed by brunch and fellowship. After the dishes were cleared, we sat in a circle again to read and discuss scripture and to ask one another our customary question, "How has God been working in your life this past week?" The habit of answering that question aloud to others helped me in many of the practices discussed in earlier chapters: becoming more self-aware, focusing on gratitude, listening to the other people, and especially listening to my inner guidance.

Other people can be particularly helpful as we try to discern what is really our inner guidance and what is fear or insecurity. As I mentioned in chapter 3, Quakers often ask a small group to help a person with discernment, the way Timothy Olsen's Episcopal congregation did. Quakers call this a clearness committee, and its work is: to seek God's guidance, not human answers; to listen deeply to the person in need of clearness; to ask questions that will help that person listen inwardly; and to refrain from giving advice. The hope is that by listening together, a group of people can hear the Truth more clearly than one person alone.

HOW TO HOLD A
CLEARNESS COMMITTEE

Clearness committees work best when you are considering a specific question like, "Am I being led to apply to graduate school?" as opposed to something vague like "What should I do with my life?" After you can articulate your question, select three or four people whose wisdom you respect. If you belong to a congregation, you might ask its help in identifying people willing to serve. Don't invite those with a vested interest in your decision, like a spouse or a business partner, though you may want to invite people who have experience with the issue you are considering. For example, if you are thinking about adopting, having some parents, preferably some adoptive parents, might be helpful, though the main criterion is that the people will help you hear your inner guidance. If the concept of a clearness committee is new to the group, you can share this outline with them ahead of time so they know what is expected.

A few weeks before the group meets, write out a summary of your dilemma, the question you are trying to answer, and any relevant background information that will help your committee know what to ask. This exercise itself may give you new insight. Distribute your summary to your committee at least a week before your meeting, which should be scheduled for a time when no one is in a hurry.

Allow at least two hours, though some groups plan for two and a half or even three hours to be on the safe side.

The group should gather in a quiet, comfortable place where it will not be interrupted. A person appointed as convener explains that the purpose of the group is to listen and ask supportive questions, not to give advice. This is often the hardest part for committee members, for people naturally want to share their own experiences and ideas, though these are usually distracting. After reviewing the guidelines, Quakers usually begin with several minutes of centering silent worship, though in Timothy's Episcopal group, it is common to begin with a spoken prayer before five to ten minutes of silence. After the silence you, the focus person, can begin by reviewing your dilemma, adding any new insights that have come since writing your summary. The group listens for important themes that need further exploration and asks questions as they arise. At any point you can deflect a question if it feels irrelevant or too personal, though it is worth taking note of what makes you uncomfortable in case there is something there that needs to be explored. It is helpful if the committee members trust their own intuitions about what needs to be asked, allowing the group to settle into silence between questions when necessary.

When it feels like the meeting has almost run its course, committee members can make nonjudgmental observations, like "I noticed that your face really lit up when you spoke about graduate school," or "You seemed to get teary when

> you shared your fears about money." You can reflect on any-
> thing that you've realized during the meeting or any next
> steps you'd like to pursue. Sometimes a next step is for the
> group to meet again, though this is not always necessary.
> Sometimes a seed will be planted during the committee that
> takes time to germinate, and it will be some time before the
> usefulness of it is clear. Reflecting on his own experience,
> both as a focus person and as a committee member, Timo-
> thy notes, "Prayer, silence, and deep listening are really
> the keys."

Hollister Knowlton found a clearness committee very helpful at an important point in her journey toward becoming a full-time advocate for sustainable living. Hollister had been volunteering with Quaker Earthcare Witness, a faith-based environmental group that was sending four delegates to the 2002 World Summit on Sustainable Development in Johannesburg, where representatives of governments from around the world would be hammering out environmental policies. When one of the Quaker delegates had to back out at short notice, Hollister was asked to go. She thought it sounded incredibly exciting, but she had never imagined herself in an international role and wondered, "Am I the right person for this?"

A friend suggested she call a clearness committee, so she quickly assembled a group of people familiar with the work she was already doing. "They just let me tell my story, and they sat and listened," recalls Hollister. She explained that she didn't know how the UN worked, so her committee asked if the other delegates did. Whenever she stated a reservation, they questioned why she felt that way. "While they didn't say, 'Well, we think you should go,' somehow by the end of the clearness committee, I felt silly for even having thought that I shouldn't go. But I loved that it was not other people advising me or telling me. They asked me questions, which helped me look at what I was saying in a different way." In another piece of serendipity, the deadlines for two grants were only a few days after the clearness committee met. Hollister had just enough time to write a proposal so that half her costs were covered, another case of way opening.

Help with discernment may be particularly important when way doesn't open quickly or easily. Timothy's group met regularly for over a year while he was testing his call, and was very supportive afterward, which was an important part of his healing. He recalls a time recently when he was asked to serve as part of someone else's discernment group and said yes before he knew the details of what the person was facing. When he realized the group was going to stir up some of his own past pain, he got angry with God for putting him in this position. "Eventually I felt the voice saying, 'Well, you were called to do this because of your experiences, and if you pray, I'll be there, and you'll be very helpful.' When I got there, I found that indeed the issues were there. The potential for pain on my part was real, but the Spirit moved through us all, and we were able to provide comfort to the focus person."

Sometimes we need comfort or encouragement, and sometimes we need to have someone to challenge our assumptions. Clearness committees can serve this function, as can spiritual directors or spiritual friends. Tom Volkert experienced this nearly fifteen years ago when he went on a thirty-day silent retreat at a desert monastery where the only person he spoke to was a spiritual director. After sixteen years as a Roman Catholic priest, Tom was beginning to question his vocation. He loved serving people and working with a community, but he also had a deep longing for marriage and family that was impossible in his current role. When he confessed this to the spiritual director on the second day, the priest said that the ability to live a celibate life was a gift from God. "If you don't have the gift, God may have helped you along this far, but don't assume He will forever." This comment shook Tom to his core, forcing him to ask himself if he was being called to leave the priesthood.

Tom took more than a year to reach a final decision. After the thirty-day silent retreat, he spent a semester at a spiritual study center, took a temporary assignment in a new parish, and then took a leave of absence. Throughout he read scripture and spiritual books, paid attention to his dreams, talked to spiritual directors, prayed, and waited. Although many signs were pointing him in a new direction, he struggled with his inner guidance because he didn't want to let other people down. After several months of this, he visited a priest friend who had been a mentor in seminary. When this mentor seemed open to the new direction Tom was considering, it took a huge weight off him, freeing him to make the decision to leave—and eventually to become my husband.

Many people need encouragement when facing a new direction. If you are afraid of disappointing people you care about, having people who encourage you can be enormously important.

The same is true if you are worried that you don't know enough to take on a new challenge or won't be able to make the grade. While a clearness committee or spiritual director should not blindly encourage anything a person wants to do, questioning whether their reservations come from the Spirit or their own insecurity can be very helpful. Through their encouragement, Hollister's and Timothy's groups helped them find the courage to take the next step, and in Timothy's case, to deal with the disappointment that followed. Supportive fellow discerners can help us challenge the source of our inner guidance, as well as ultimately trust it.

Spiritual community should be a place that helps us become more of our True Selves. Many of the people in chapter 1 went searching for a new faith community because they didn't feel true to themselves or connected to God in the place where they were. For Melvin Metelits, finding spiritual community meant coming back to Judaism after nearly five decades of rejecting it. "In our Jewish path, God's voice can be heard through an individual, but it's more likely to be heard through study of Torah, and through community and tradition," explains Melvin, who now teaches Torah and tells spiritual stories. The serenity he now feels about his life could not have come in isolation, without other people who were also struggling to understand God's teachings.

Many people have their spirits nurtured outside of organized religion, but still find that community is important to their development. Will Brock grew up in a small town where becoming a musician felt like a pipe dream until he went to a high school for the performing arts. "All of a sudden, I saw hundreds of kids just like me," recalls Will. "It made me see for the first time, 'Oh, I

don't have to be alone.' That's like an amazing epiphany to realize that you're not by yourself in the way that you think." From
that point on, Will had a new determination to make his dream
a reality. Today collaborating with other musicians is an essential
part of his work. As Will points out, it can be empowering to
realize that you are not alone in the way you think. In contrast, it
can be discouraging, even depressing, to feel isolated and strange.
This was a challenge for Hollister, who in her twenties was married to an investment banker, which put her into a social circle
that did not value simple living. It was only after her divorce that
she was able to change her own lifestyle to make it more sustainable. Finding a congregation that included people who shared
these values further empowered her.

Sometimes observing where you fit in socially can help you
discover who you are, as I realized one day during my senior
year of college. Although I had spent most of my undergradu-
ate years' studying world religions and cultures and had studied
abroad twice, as graduation approached I started to panic about
my financial future. Being the first person in my immediate family to go to college, I wondered if I should go make a lot of money
instead of looking for service opportunities overseas, which was
what interested me most. One day I was in the career placement
office, wearing my new navy suit with matching heels to meet
with a recruiter from a Wall Street firm. Immediately afterward
I would be meeting with a recruiter from the Peace Corps. As I
waited, I looked at the interview schedules hanging on the wall
and noticed that I had several friends on the Peace Corps list, but
none on the investment banker list. It felt like a sign about where
I belonged. During the interviews, I felt much more comfortable,

more myself, with the Peace Corps recruiter, even though I was grossly overdressed. When I was invited for a second interview on Wall Street, I felt like a sham, a feeling that helped me see that was not the career for me. Teaching in an African village was much more in harmony with who I really was.

SERENITY AND COURAGE

Becoming a Peace Corps volunteer in Botswana gave me a very different understanding of community. In my village, if one neighbor owned an ax and another a wheelbarrow, they shared their tools, making little distinction about who owned what. If a woman was cooking dinner and realized she was out of onions, she asked her neighbor for an onion, whereas most of the westerners in my village would put on their sun hats and walk a mile in the scorching heat to the village store. When I finally caught on and started relying on my African neighbors, they were delighted. I realized that the unwillingness of most whites to ask for help was seen as a weakness, rather than as a strength. While self-sufficiency is highly valued in the United States, interdependence is at the core of Tswana culture. Africans often asked me if it was true that in America we put our elders in institutions, away from extended family, a concept that seemed incongruous to people for whom connections to other people were foundational.

Educator Joan Countryman explains the African concept of *ubuntu*, which implies that "who I am is shaped by my relationship to other human beings." It is related to traditional African spirituality and the sense that we are all interconnected, including with our ancestors. Joan says she could see how this belief was part of the school she ran in South Africa, as well as in the wider country. "One of the things that is very attractive about South Africa is that they are consciously trying to build a new community," notes Joan. "They are saying, 'We have this horrible past, but we are going to try to build a community where people look after each other.' " She recalls one day when the government was presenting the budget on television, and her students watched with great interest. "It was a big event," she recalls, laughing because nobody in the United States would want to watch budget hearings, least of all students. In contrast, the South African girls had many ideas about the budget. "That was true of the whole country," Joan notes, adding that it may be because democracy is so new there. "There was this sense that 'I'm connected to this, and it's important that I know about it.' "

Joan feels her own society could use this sense of connection. Since working for Oprah Winfrey, Joan is trying to use her new limelight to advocate for education whenever she is asked to speak publicly. "What I'm trying to get people to think about is that we all need to care about education. It isn't a matter of, 'Well, I don't have children,' or 'I don't have children in public school.' " Such individualism, she feels, has helped lead to schools that are depressing places of little learning. "Why would you want to live in this community if the police don't have access to good education?" she asks. "All of our lives would be better if we addressed this concern for everybody."

Unfortunately, there are aspects of contemporary American culture that make it easy to feel separate from other people. As Tracey Smith-Diggs pointed out in chapter 4, the evening news fuels our fear of crime, sometimes out of all proportion. Being dependent on our automobiles makes many North Americans isolated in a way my Botswana neighbors never were. Because of the zoning rules that Hollister Knowlton described in chapter 3, we might drive in one direction to worship, in another to take our children to school, and another for work. As a result, we might be part of multiple communities, without feeling fully part of any of them. The advent of electronic devices hasn't helped. When my son was seven he complained about not having anyone to talk to at his summer camp on the daily bus ride to the pool. When I asked why, he explained that all his friends were listening to their iPods.

Of course this is not true everywhere. Local cultures have their own distinct flavor, and some have stronger communities than others. Ro'Bin points out that she sees a big difference between the culture of New Orleans and that of the urban North, and not just in terms of the gumbo and jazz. "I have a next-door neighbor now, and I don't know her name," notes Ro'Bin. "That's normal here, but at home we know who Miss Rose is down the street and Grandpa Diggs's whole family. We knew who our neighbors were." In New Orleans if Ro'Bin needed a ride somewhere, she had five sisters and a brother she could call, but in the North she doesn't have that social support. Unfortunately Ro'Bin's new experience is becoming more common than it was a few generations ago. Martin Seligman, author of *Learned Optimism*, notes: "Individual failure used to be buffered by the second force, the large 'we.' . . . Faith in God, community, nation, and the large extended family have all eroded in the last forty years, and the spiritual furniture that we used to sit in has become threadbare."

If Timothy Olsen had not had a supportive community to embrace him in his time of disappointment and injury, he would have had a much more difficult time letting go of his anger and coming to a place of peace. Likewise for Dan Gottlieb. Eileen Smith would have felt much more anxious caring for her mother alone, if she didn't have neighbors and friends giving her support. Matthew Cole might not have stayed sober through his divorce. This is not criticism of those individuals, but a simple acknowledgment that we need other people to support us in difficult times. Not having enough social support decreases our ability to accept with serenity the things we cannot change.

Disconnection from other people also makes it more difficult for us to find the courage to change what should be changed, especially in terms of larger societal issues. I recall a cartoon that depicted a large crowd of people standing side by side, each with a bubble over their head that said, "One person can't make a difference." Each person felt disempowered, though collectively they could have done much. As the old union song goes, "Many stones can build an arch, singly none, singly none." That was the lesson of the union movement. If one coal miner asks for a raise or safer working conditions, he'll be laughed at or fired; but when all the workers ask together, they are much more likely to get what they want.

What keeps us from banding together to change more of the things that could be changed if we worked collectively? Many writers have noted that the individualism of our culture can be one barrier to collective action. Rabbi Michael Lerner—an activist, psychologist, and the editor of *Tikuun* magazine—argues that our tendency to see all our problems as personal, rather than seeing how they are part of larger social patterns, keeps us from identifying real solutions. He argues that "Communities of Compassion"—where people honestly share their stories—are part of the solution: "We will never realistically know ourselves until we know how much of what we perceive as unique and personal to ourselves is actually the shared experience of all those around us," writes Lerner. "Nor will we ever be able to build a movement for social change until we can hear the pain of others."

Just as individuals may have to face their social conditioning to find wisdom, so groups of people can face their cultural assumptions and change them, thus changing the world. The wisdom to know the difference is something we need as individuals, but it's also something we need as a society. As I pointed out in the introduction, Reinhold Niebuhr's version of the Serenity Prayer was written in the plural and asks for the courage to change what should be changed, rather than only what can be changed, which challenges us to consider how we might work together to make the world a better place.

Evangelical minister and writer Jim Wallis believes that the United States is in the midst of a cultural transformation. In *The Great Awakening*, he argues that there is a religious revival happening, similar to the ones that led to the abolition of slavery and the civil rights movement: "Faith is being applied to social justice in ways that we might have never imagined just a few short years ago. Spiritual power is being harnessed to address the greatest social challenges that we face today." These social challenges include things like global poverty and a new, less domineering relationship to the earth, issues that need many people working together. Wallis is optimistic that the conditions are ripe for major efforts. "Each new generation has a chance to alter two basic definitions of reality in our world—what is acceptable and what is possible," writes Wallis. History shows, he argues, that when people change their definitions of what is acceptable and what is possible, tangible change follows.

The civil rights movement redefined the culture of the United States. There had always been people who criticized Jim Crow laws. There were individuals who broke the unjust laws in protest at least as far back as 1892, when Homer Plessy, a biracial man from New Orleans, sat in a white's only train car to protest segregation on the rails. Before Rosa Parks, there were others—mostly blacks, but also a few whites—who refused to sit where they were told. There were many more like Joan Countryman's parents, who left the South or packed their own lunches to avoid the indignity of discrimination. So why is Rosa Parks the famous one? Because Rosa Parks was part of a movement, one that organized a bus boycott when she was arrested for refusing to move to the back of the bus in 1955.

Originally the demand of the Montgomery bus boycott was for a more polite segregation policy on the buses. Doing away with separate seating altogether was a change that didn't seem possible. When the boycott gained widespread support, however, the organizers raised their expectations and demanded total desegregation. Throughout the movement they exemplified Jim Wallis's point, that things changed once large numbers of people redefined what was acceptable and what was possible. Conscience-led people of different backgrounds working together broke unjust laws both to undermine those laws and to raise public debate through their willingness to risk arrest, attack, and even death. Not only did the movement succeed in overturning legalized segregation and discrimination, it also showed the world that committed, collective action could have dramatic results, a lesson that helped inspire freedom-seeking people around the world, as well as the antiwar movement that followed in the United States.

An immigrant from Ireland to the United States, Father Michael Doyle became convinced during the 1960s that the Vietnam War was unacceptable. "You just couldn't square it with the Sermon on the Mount," he explains, referring to the Gospel passage where Jesus tells his followers to "Love your enemies" and "Turn the other cheek." In the 1960s, speaking out against the war in the New Jersey Catholic school where he taught only got Father Michael transferred to a parish in Camden, a poor neighborhood where he watched young men whose families could not afford college drafted into the army and sometimes returned home in body bags. Feeling that writing letters or preaching against the war was not enough, he took inspiration from Catholic priests like brothers Daniel and Philip Berrigan, who changed the definition of what was possible for priests by destroying draft board records to hinder the government's ability to send more young Americans to Vietnam. When Father Michael learned that local activists were planning to break into the Camden draft board, he joined what became known as the Camden 28, which included three other Roman Catholic priests and a protestant minister.

Unbeknownst to the group, one of their members was an informant for the FBI, which secretly funded and encouraged the break-in plan so it could swoop in and make public arrests. When Father Michael and his colleagues were caught in the act of ripping up draft records, they each faced a possible forty-seven years in jail. Being together gave them the courage to refuse a plea deal that would have greatly reduced the charges. Instead they made the trial into a referendum on the war and the FBI's tactics, making their acquittal a victory for the antiwar movement. Obviously that alone did not lead to the end of the war, but it was one of many actions by many groups across the country that pressured the U.S. government to change its policy. In the brogue of his native Ireland, Father Michael compares collective effort to a rope that is made up of many thin threads that together can pull a ship. "Community is strengthening," he notes, explaining that he was too timid to have had the courage to break into the draft board by himself. "There is nothing that bonds people more than risk together," he adds, comparing it to the brotherhood men feel in war. "If I meet any one of the Camden 28 today, it's like a celebration."

There is a special sense of power and excitement that can come from working with others. Just think of the pictures of joyous Germans dismantling the Berlin Wall one chop at a time. If any one of them had dared to take a sledgehammer to the wall even a short time before, they would have surely been shot dead, but when everyone worked together, the previously unimaginable became a reality.

Group effort does not always need to be dangerous or controversial to make a difference. Recently I attended a weekend retreat near Pittsburgh where fifty-some participants had come from different parts of the United States. On the first evening, a woman who had flown from Alaska shared how guilty she felt about the environmental impact of her long flight and how she had thought of giving a donation to a green building project as a "carbon offset"—a way of balancing the carbon dioxide released as a result of her trip with something that would reduce greenhouse gases. She said she felt led to invite others in the group to make similar donations, depending on how far and by what means they had traveled. The group took up the idea, though it rejected the assumption that those who had come the farthest should pay the most. Instead people helped the woman who raised the concern to calculate the total carbon cost of our group's travel through a website designed for that purpose. It turned out that because most people had driven, instead of flown, and many had carpooled, we had released much less carbon than the woman had initially assumed. Many of us had in fact been mindful of the environment in our travel plans, though we didn't have any sense of it making a difference until we calculated our impact as a group. By putting out a plastic bucket on the last day of the retreat, we were able to raise more than the amount suggested by the website and donate it to the green building project. There was a sense that making this witness as a group was much more powerful than if each of us had sent a check individually.

In recent years many ordinary people have been quietly changing the way they see their responsibility toward the earth. On a train ride several months ago, I heard an Amtrak worker and an elderly passenger talking about how they'd both stopped leaving their cell phones plugged in overnight, so as not to waste electricity. They seemed to be happy to discover they were not alone, which they are not. *The New York Times* reports that groups of "eco-moms" are meeting to discuss how they can reduce their carbon emissions. Universities are reducing their environmental impact, often with the encouragement of students, as are businesses, from my favorite coffee shop to Walmart. Knowing that we are not alone can encourage us to do more than we would if we had the illusion of isolation.

With scientists predicting major climate changes on the horizon, Hollister Knowlton feels urgency about her work, but also hope. She shares an analogy she's heard, that humanity is like a caterpillar that devours a tremendous amount. When it has eaten enough, spontaneously "imaginal cells" appear in its body. They are a relatively small number of cells, but somehow they migrate until they find one another. It is only when the imaginal cells reach a critical mass that the caterpillar is transformed into a pupa, the stage before becoming a butterfly. "There are imaginal cells all over like me, like Thomas Berry, like Joanna Macy," she explains, referring to two famous environmental writers. "We are beginning to find each other." Hollister recalls a conference where Paul Hawken showed a video scrolling the names of all the organizations around the world that were working on sustainability issues. The author of *Blessed Unrest: How the Largest Movement in the World Came into Being and Why No One Saw It Coming*, Hawken told the audience that there were so many organizations that if he had started the tape on Friday evening and ran it all weekend through to Monday, they still would not have finished the list. "So the tape speeded up," recalls Hollister. "This is a movement. This is not something that started from the top. This is bubbling up from below. Joanna Macy calls this the Great Turning. She says, 'There is no guarantee we can pull it off, but if we don't try, what is there?'"

Practicing Wisdom Together

Even when people work together, major change is not quick or easy. Many people who say that our reduction of carbon emissions must be faster and more dramatic in order to avoid catastrophic consequences feel impatient that their society is not changing enough. They are forced to accept the fact that not everyone sees things their way, even within their own communities. In fact, because we seek support and empowerment from our communities, divisions within them can be painful, giving us opportunities to practice the lessons discussed in previous chapters: acceptance of other people, forgiveness, and discernment, as well as being true to ourselves. For this reason, community can be a challenging but fruitful training ground for wisdom.

While it is easy to romanticize some of the historic groups that have facilitated social change, in truth many of them were rife with personal and ideological divisions that were agonizing for the people involved. The betrayal of the Camden 28 is but one example. Like the rest of those who planned the break-in at the Camden draft board in 1971, Bob Hardy strongly opposed the Vietnam War, though he had reservations about the ethics of civil disobedience. Bob decided to tell the FBI of the group's plans, not out of a desire to harm his friends, but out of a desire to stop them from breaking the law, which is what the FBI claimed to want, as well. The FBI promised Bob that it had no intention of prosecuting the group, a promise that was broken as soon as the arrests were made. "Bob thought he could handle anything, but the FBI played him," says Father Michael, who was Bob's parish priest.

While on one level this was a political drama, played out in the newspapers, it was also a painful break between friends and within a parish community. Dealing with that human aspect intensified when Bob Hardy's nine-year-old son had a tragic accident, falling from a tree onto a spiked fence. Father Michael recalls going to the hospital to visit the Hardy family and finding himself sitting on a couch with Bob and an FBI agent, a situation that seemed unreal to Father Michael, who was still angry about the betrayal. "I was twisted inside out," he remembers. Father Michael decided that to really be a peacemaker he had to put their human connection above their political differences. When Bob's son died three weeks after his accident, Father Michael led the funeral mass, which was attended by most of the Camden 28.

In the decades since their trial, Father Michael has attended the funerals of many participants, including several defendants, a juror, and the judge. A few years ago, when Father Michael heard that the prosecutor had died, he debated whether he should travel two hours to the funeral. "If I go and it doesn't really matter, I'll enjoy the train ride," he thought. "But if I don't go and I should have gone, then I can never do anything about it." His decision to go was affirmed after the funeral when the prosecutor's widow went out of her way to shake hands with him. "She said, 'He really loved you,'" recalls Father Michael, adding that he was an extremely argumentative witness during the trial who made the prosecutor's work difficult. "She was delighted that I came, and she gave money to support a film on the Camden 28. I felt I was ten feet tall, going out the door. Did I do the right thing, or what? You talk about forgiveness and healing. It was amazing."

Although Father Michael is outspoken in his views, he notes, "I never met anybody worthy of my hate. What I mean is I don't want to do that to myself. That's too much for me to give away. I've got enough flaws myself. Everybody's flawed. One of the great promises is what Jesus said: 'Judge not, and ye shall not be judged.' That's a good deal," he notes. Indeed, we all have flaws, and community has a way of bringing them out. Working with other people can give us opportunities to see our own flaws and also opportunities to practice forgiveness when we encounter the imperfections and insecurities of others. Although these opportunities may not always be welcome, over time they can help us develop wisdom and patience.

After more than thirty-five years of living and working in community, Eileen Smith says, "The most important lesson I've learned is to keep my mouth shut. As I've aged, I've learned that listening is the most important part of community: listening to other people, listening to yourself, and listening to God." She confesses with a laugh, "I'm kind of rigid in my opinions. So when I go into meetings where there is going to be an outcome, I have a thought in mind about what the outcome should be. I'm kind of ashamed to say this, but if I want something badly enough, I'll try to manipulate the group a little bit to get them to see things my way. Life has taught me that I really need to soften my will, and listening is the only way I know how to do that."

Being part of a community can help you soften your will and practice letting go because communities inevitably include disagreements. If you accept that each person has a spark of Truth, then listening for different pieces of the truth can broaden your perspective. This can be a powerful practice for groups of people seeking God's guidance together. As Timothy Olsen said of discernment groups, "Prayer, silence, and deep listening are really the keys." This description also applies to larger groups seeking divine guidance, like Quaker congregations, which make all decisions through a group discernment process. We are not immune from the problem Eileen describes—strong-willed people trying to get their own way—but we come together with the hope that we can let go of our own wills and seek God's will. Although it doesn't always happen, sometimes we experience a profound sense of being guided as a group, often bringing us to a solution that no one person could have imagined alone.

One of my most memorable experiences of group discernment occurred six months after the terrorist attacks of September 11, 2001. Quakers in my city of Philadelphia were grappling with how to advocate for peace in the face of terrorism and the war on terrorism. With this in mind, the regional Quaker body, Philadelphia Yearly Meeting, had invited Palestinian Quaker Jean Zaru, a longtime advocate for peace and justice in the Middle East, to give a keynote speech at our four-day annual meeting. During her talk on the opening night, Jean spoke of the difficulty she experienced traveling from Ramallah to Philadelphia and of her struggle to work for justice nonviolently. She spoke of all people being interconnected and of the need for compassion. During the question-and-answer session, someone asked about the condition of her congregation and the audience learned of the desperate straits faced by Ramallah Friends Meeting. In the face of roadblocks and violence, their numbers had dwindled. Their historic meetinghouse was on the verge of collapse with no resources to repair it.

"Jean was very clear that she was not coming here to ask for money," explains Arlene Kelly, who clerked (or facilitated) the annual meeting. Still, many present were moved by Jean's presentation. A few leaders put together a proposal to help Ramallah Friends rebuild their roof before the rest of the building collapsed, and the proposal was brought before the body of a few hundred people thirty-six hours after Jean's speech. "More than with any other session the feeling was, 'What is really the leading of the Spirit?' " recalls Arlene. The response from the group was overwhelmingly positive. Although financial discussions could often be contentious, the group easily approved giving $50,000 to save the meetinghouse, but with the added proviso that they didn't want the action to be purely financial. If way opened, Philadelphia Quakers asserted their hope that they could enter into a spiritual partnership with the Palestinian Quakers that would be mutually enriching. "It was a very deeply moving emotional time for me," says Arlene.

In the wake of that session, with the escalation of the second *intifada*, violence increased in Ramallah, and Jean's return was delayed. "It seemed very foolish under the circumstances to start putting money into the meetinghouse," admits Arlene. Still, she and others had a sense that it was what they were called to do, and way did open, despite many challenges. Word spread, and many people came forward with additional contributions, from local young children to other regional Quaker groups, like Baltimore Yearly Meeting. On the Palestinian end, an experienced construction manager agreed to take on the job, and local laborers were grateful to work at a time when there was little work available. As the meetinghouse was gradually rebuilt in central

Ramallah, local people began to see it as a symbol of hope amid all the destruction.

When the building was rededicated—coincidentally on the ninety-fifth anniversary of its original dedication—the ceremony was attended by supporters from the United States, as well as Jews, Muslims, and Christians from the region. Since then, the meetinghouse and its annex, which was also rebuilt, have become a place where Muslims and Jews can meet, where people of differing political views can gather for discussion, and where people of any faith are welcome to worship. A program coordinator has been hired, someone whom Arlene had initially imagined as the perfect person for the job, though at the time Arlene assumed she would be unavailable. "I'm always suspicious when people say, 'Well, things worked out, so that proves God was behind it,'" says Arlene. "But there is a sense that the Spirit has been at work and that the climate for us to move forward has been hospitable." Arlene confesses that on her way to the rededication ceremony, she thought, "Who do we think we are? How do we have the audacity to think we can do anything?" But she says her experience there has given her hope that, although they cannot solve all the huge problems, it was right for them to change what they could.

A retired therapist, Arlene continues to be involved with the Ramallah project, though she spends much of her time deepening and strengthening spiritual communities closer to home. She says that the conditions that help communities discern are the same as for individuals. "Know yourself," she advises. "If it is a community, there has to be some glue, something that is shared, and I think that is the basis of the discernment." When Arlene is working with groups she encourages them to use the word "community" very seriously and points out that thirty people together in a room don't make a community.

Groups may have to examine themselves from time to time to be sure they know what their "glue" is. They have to define their mission, just like individuals, or risk getting out of their lane. AA does not endorse causes, political candidates, or books like this one. One could argue that AA should lobby for more money for alcohol treatment, but lobbying would distract it from its primary purpose, helping people become and stay sober. A lobbying organization, in contrast, might get distracted if it started dabbling in direct service.

Sacred Heart has a clear mission: to be a place where the poor are honored. Father Michael's parish since before the Camden 28 trial, Sacred Heart church sits amid desolate streets, near a putrid sewage treatment plant. "It's a terrible place to live," says Father Michael, "but it's a great place for a parish." He explains that their work is clear, comparing it to the work of a parent who is near a crying child. "You don't need to do much discerning if you stay near the need. What we often do is separate ourselves from the need," moving to the suburbs, leaving the poor in a warehouse of poverty, "and then you don't hear their cry," he says. "So at Sacred Heart we come near the need." He adds, "If you break bread on Sunday, you better be breaking it on Monday, too."

"Breaking bread" is a potent symbol in the Christian tradition for the meeting of God and one another through communion. Of his city, Father Michael observes, "When you look at the tragedy of this place, the only spot within about four blocks that you could purchase something to eat is a Chinese place with a hole in the wall where you put your money in and the food comes out. It's totally lacking in human respect." In contrast, Sacred Heart tries to make their food sharing program a place of dignity that includes prayer and singing. "If my mother had to come for food, she wouldn't be belittled," he explains. The parish also runs a thrift shop where diapers are sold below cost, and good children's clothes are affordable. Though most Catholics have left the neighborhood, they run a school because it serves an obvious need in a community where the public schools are terrible. "The people will let us know when they don't want it because they won't come," explains Father Michael. "As long as they're knocking, we'll keep it going. Again, it didn't need a lot of effort to find what we should do."

Father Michael combines infectious hope with brutal realism, something that clearly comes from his faith. "Our religion is based on the success of failure," he explains. "The whole thing about Christ is that he had done all he could, he had given his life, and he ended up executed publicly in front of his mother. Imagine that ending for a life—in the most public, brutal way of the Roman Empire. And it exploded into redemption, or solution." The lesson, he says, is "Change what should be changed, even though it looks impossible. Maybe it won't work, but just go for it. Don't be so quick to say it cannot be done."

Queries

Do you have a community that encourages your spiritual growth?

If not, is that something you wish for?

Who are the people who challenge you and give you practice with forgiveness?

Who are the people who help you see who you are more clearly?

What are the things you are forced to accept about your community?

What would you like to change about your community?

What would you change in the wider world if you had a movement of people behind you?

Have you ever experienced God at work among a group of people acting together?

Conclusion

WISDOM

Michael Doyle and Dan Gottlieb—two men whom I respect and like very much—each emphasize different lines of the Serenity Prayer. Accept everything, says Dr. Dan, live there for a long time, and then you'll be able to see what you can change. Father Michael, on the other hand, says you should change what should be changed, even when it seems impossible. Only after you've done your best should you accept that there are things you can't change. So which one is articulating the wisdom to know the difference?

The discrepancy in their approaches comes partly from the two men's temperaments and life experiences, and partly from the fact that they are focused on different kinds of problems. Dan's job is to listen to the suffering of the human heart. As a family therapist, he hears the ways that people's expectations create their own suffering, and so he emphasizes acceptance, the lesson life has taught him so profoundly. Michael, on the other hand, sees the suffering created by the economic gap between his poor neighbors and his more affluent parishioners, and he knows it is not good for our souls to passively accept the misery of our neighbors. Furthermore, while Dan ministers to individuals, who can only change themselves, Michael ministers to a community, which has the power to change much more. Despite their differences, they both exemplify wisdom.

The Dalai Lama made a distinction between a natural calamity, which can only be accepted, and a problem created by human misunderstanding, which can and should be corrected. While this insight is a helpful starting place in discerning the difference between what we can and cannot change, in truth many challenges contain aspects of both. Hurricane Katrina, which swept the Gulf Coast of the United States in 2005, was certainly a natural calamity, but wider recognition of its power by both government officials and citizens would have reduced the amount of suffering that followed. Many people have been forced to accept that the lives they once knew were washed away, but accepting the hurricane does not mean we as a society have to settle for the dreadful government response to the storm. We can't change the past, but we are not powerless about the future. As a society, we can prepare for future relief efforts and build stronger levees. We can learn from past mistakes and make sure we don't make them again. In fact, learning from our mistakes is one of the best ways to develop wisdom.

While psychologists have not come up with a universally agreed-on definition of wisdom, they have been studying it, with some interesting results. Several qualities seem to be common among people who score high on tests designed to measure wisdom. According to an overview of such studies, wise people "learn from previous negative experiences. They are able to step outside themselves and assess a troubling situation with calm reflection. They recast a crisis as a problem to be addressed, a puzzle to be solved. They take action in situations they can control and accept the inability to do so when matters are outside their control." In other words, wise people do not necessarily avoid difficulties, but they do make the best of them.

It sounds so simple. So what gets in the way of wisdom? Fear is the biggest culprit. Belief in a narrow, judging God can make us afraid of life itself. Likewise, fear of inner guidance that goes against cultural norms can keep us from listening to it or make us afraid to let others see our True Selves. Fear can get in the way of compassion, gratitude, and seeing the goodness in other people, which in turn can make our relationships more difficult. Fear makes us cling to a picture of how we think things should be, making acceptance of what is almost impossible. By separating people, fear undermines community, depriving us of its power. In short, fear makes us go through life with our guard up, wasting energy that could be put to better use. In contrast, both serenity and courage are based on living with trust.

Learning to live with trust does not happen overnight, just as the spiritual practices in this book are not necessarily learned in a neat progression: recognize your conditioning, know yourself, then listen for divine guidance and change your attitude. Instead they are points around a spiral. Each practice makes the others easier. Accepting yourself makes it easier to accept others. Accepting others makes it more likely you will bring out the best in them, which helps to build a strong community. Community, in turn, can help you listen to God and know yourself. Sometimes it may feel like you are going in circles, until you realize that you are a little wiser than the last time around. As Fatima bin Mustafa says, your faith grows. You are a bit more serene for the next flat tire. You can accept it, change it, and move on.

Accepting life's flat tires seems to be easier for people who have accepted themselves. If you know who you are, what you are capable of, and what you are called to do, you are much less likely to waste your time and energy sweating the small stuff or even the big stuff that you cannot change. You are less likely to project your uncomfortable feelings onto other people, instead of facing your feelings and learning what they have to teach you. You are less likely to waste time trying to change other people and more likely to influence them with a positive example. Knowing yourself, as Thomas Merton asserted, also helps you to know God and to trust that you live and work within a larger plan that you are not always able to see. A friend of mine uses the phrase "Lord, your ocean is so wide, and my boat is so small." She observes, "I've got to be in my boat, and I've got to keep paddling. But it's in this infinite ocean. I would just be ludicrous to think I knew fully and completely where I was going."

It's helpful to remember that Reinhold Niebuhr's version of the Serenity Prayer asks first for "grace." Such humility is a step toward serenity, accepting that even when we're paddling as hard as we can, we can't control the ocean. We can only control our own paddle. Likewise, a step toward courage is recognizing that our own paddle matters. After all, thousands of Katrina victims were rescued from their rooftops by people in rowboats, many of them ordinary citizens who just started rowing. Their willingness to brave the waters certainly made a difference.

NOTES

Introduction

6 "God, give us grace": Sifton, *The Serenity Prayer*, 7. On pages 292–93. Elisabeth Sifton, who is Niebuhr's daughter, makes similar observations on how the meaning of this prayer is different from the simpler version. For the controversy over whether Niebuhr was the original author, see Fred R. Shapiro, "Who Wrote the Serenity Prayer?" and Elisabeth Sifton, "It Takes a Master to Make a Masterpiece," both in *Yale Alumni Magazine*, July/August 2008, 34–41. In my opinion, whoever authored the prayer, the fact that it had such resonance during World War II confirms my sense that it has broader social implications than are often realized.

ONE: THE COURAGE TO QUESTION

21 "They are mere bad habits of thought": Seligman, *Learned Optimism*, 220.

23 "One of the things that hit me": Quoted in Jill Neimark, "What Can We Do About Suffering?" *Spirituality & Health*, May–June 2007, 69.

26 "Cultural legacies are powerful forces": Gladwell, *Outliers*, 175, 220, 237–38.

29 "There is abundant evidence": Hara Estroff Marano, *A Nation of Wimps: The High Cost of Invasive Parenting* (New York: Broadway, 2008), 7.

29 One study of a crisis: Mary Carmichael, "Who Says Stress Is Bad for You?" *Newsweek*, February 23, 2009, 48.

33 "Religion has often been a tool": Greeley, *Religion as Poetry* , 6.

37 *"You cannot control everything"*: Kurtz and Ketcham, *The Spirituality of Imperfection*, 120, 123. Emphasis in the original.

37 "It was a devastating blow to my pride": Alcoholics Anonymous, *Alcoholics Anonymous—The Big Book*, 7–8, 46.

39 A sociologist interested in the intersection of religion and culture: Greeley, *The Catholic Imagination*, 43.

TWO: KNOWING YOURSELF

52 "A man walking through the forest": Quoted in *Kurtz and Ketcham, The Spirituality of Imperfection*, 93.

53 "Everything has its own Inner Nature": Hoff, *The Tao of Pooh*, 40, 57.

55 "I think I'll go to business school": This story was previously told in Eileen Flanagan, *Listen with Your Heart: Seeking the Sacred in Romantic Love* (New York: Warner, 1999).

56 "That's no realistic goal": Malcolm X with Haley, *The Autobiography of Malcolm X,* 43.

57 Teresa of Avila, a Roman Catholic saint: Quoted in Nolan, *Jesus Today*, 101.

57 "We must recognize that nothing is more difficult to bear": Jung, *The Collected Works of C. G. Jung*, vol. 7, 223.

63 "Strangely enough we strengthen love in ourselves," O'Connor, *Our Many Selves*, xv.

66 "Why do you see the speck": Luke 6:41 (RSV).

70 "breathing is the link between our body and our mind": Hanh, *Peace Is Every Step*, 9.

71 "When you need to slow down": Hanh, *Peace Is Every Step*, 15–16.

71 "The conscious resolution to change": Keating, *Invitation to Love*, 3, 22.

THREE: SEEKING DIVINE WISDOM

86 "A call may come as a gradual dawning": Farnham et al., *Listening Hearts*, 7.

87 "I will instruct you and teach you": Psalms 32:08 (RSV).

89 "love, joy, peace, patience, kindness": Galatians 5:22–23 (RSV).

94 "The place God calls you to": Buechner, *Wishful Thinking*, 119.

106 "Though it is arrogance to say we are 'masters of our fate' ": May, *Love & Will*, 270. Emphasis in the original.

107 "Why do you cry out": This story appears in Exodus 14:13–21. Here, for consistency, I have used the "conversational" language that Lew uses.

107 "What the Torah seems to be hinting at": Lew, *Be Still and Get Going*, 126.

112 "The desire to change the world": Reginald A. Ray, "The Buddha's Politics," in McLeod, *Mindful Politics*, 67.

Four: Shifting Your Perspective

122 For example, a teacher isn't smiling: Chansky, *Freeing Your Child from Negative Thinking*, 50–51, 89–91.

134 "If you have a sense of caring for others": Tenzin Gyatso, the Dalai Lama, *The Compassionate Life*, 13–14.

137 "When you are angry with someone": Hanh, *Anger*, 55.

140 "For years my mind flashed red": Schachter-Shalomi, *From Age-ing to Sage-ing*, 94–95.

140 "Felt better about their lives": Deborah Norville, "How the New Science of Thank You Can Change Your Life," *Reader's Digest*, October 2007, 149.

144 "Buddhist practitioners familiar with the workings of the mind": The Dalai Lama, "Foreword," in Begley, *Train Your Mind, Change Your Brain*, viii.

147 "tend to get more forgetful": Jessica Ruvinsky, "For the Elderly, TV Is Harmful to Mental Health," *Yale Alumni Magazine*, September/October 2005, 23.

Five: Practicing Loving Acceptance

158 "There are occasions when the lack of understanding": Hanh, *The Art of Power*, 105.

163 "You can get rid of just about any behavior": Quoted in Carlo Rotella, "When Your Kid Whines, Screams, Hits, Kicks, and Bites—Relax," *Yale Alumni Magazine*, September/October 2005, 40–49.

166 "Instead of putting effort into making something happen": Simpkins, *Simple Taoism*, 70.

171 "You are the bows": Gibran, *The Prophet*, 18.

179 "Both overinvolvement and underinvolvement come from anxiety": All quotations from Dan Gottlieb are from my interview with him;

some background information came from his book *Learning from the Heart*.

SIX: LETTING GO OF OUTCOMES

199 "Over the years that I have been interviewing": Weil, *Spontaneous Healing*, 88, 100.

200 "They accept the diagnosis": Quoted in Hirshberg and Barasch, *Remarkable Recovery*, 302.

203 "the deepest reason why we are afraid of death": Sogyal Rinpoche, *The Tibetan Book of Living and Dying*, 15, 20.

205 "Does man have any role": "... Thy Will Be Done?" *60 Minutes*, February 1, 1998.

209 "Death is nothing to resist": Ostrom, *In God We Die*.

211 "are often seen as not spiritual enough": bell hooks, "Buddhism and the Politics of Domination," in McLeod, *Mindful Politics*, 59.

211 "Of the many problems we face today": The Dalai Lama, "A New Approach to Global Problems," in McLeod, *Mindful Politics*, 17.

SEVEN: FINDING WISDOM IN COMMUNITY

221 "All shall be well": Julian of Norwich, *Revelations of Divine Love*, 69.

237 "Individual failure used to be buffered": Seligman, *Learned Optimism*, vi.

239 "We will never realistically know ourselves": Lerner, *Surplus Powerlessness*, 339–40.

239 "Faith is being applied to social justice": Wallis, *The Great Awakening*, 1, 286.

241 Unbeknownst to the group: All quotations are from my interview with Michael Doyle. A few background details are from Anthony

Giacchino's documentary *The Camden 28* (First Run Features, 2007).

Conclusion: Wisdom

257 "learn from previous negative experiences": Stephen S. Hall, "The Older-and-Wiser Hypothesis," *The New York Times Magazine*, May 6, 2007, 63, 66.

BIBLIOGRAPHY

Alcoholics Anonymous. *Alcoholics Anonymous—The Big Book*, 4th ed. New York: Alcoholics Anonymous World Services, 2001.

———. *Twelve Steps and Twelve Traditions*. New York: Alcoholics Anonymous World Services, 2002.

Armstrong, Karen. *The Battle for God*. New York: Alfred A. Knopf, 2000.

Begley, Sharon. *Train Your Mind, Change Your Brain: How a New Science Reveals Our Extraordinary Potential to Transform Ourselves*. New York: Ballantine Books, 2007.

Buechner, Frederick. *Wishful Thinking: A Seeker's ABC*. San Francisco: HarperSanFrancisco, 1993.

Chansky, Tamar E. *Freeing Your Child from Negative Thinking: Powerful, Practical Strategies to Build a Lifetime of Resilience, Flexibility, and Happiness*. Philadelphia: Perseus, 2008.

Chopra, Deepak. *The Essential How to Know God: The Essence of the Soul's Journey into the Mystery of Mysteries*. New York: Harmony Books, 2000.

Elam, Jennifer. *Dancing with God Through the Storm: Mysticism and Mental Illness*. Media, PA: Way Opens, 2002.

Farnham, Suzanne G., et al. *Listening Hearts: Discerning Call in Community*. Harrisburg, PA: Morehouse, 1991.

Farrington, Debra K. *Hearing with the Heart: A Gentle Guide to Discerning God's Will for Your Life*. San Francisco: Jossey-Bass, 2003.

Fox, George. *The Journal of George Fox*. Edited by John L. Nickalls. London: London Yearly Meeting, 1975.

Gibran, Kahlil. *The Prophet*. New York: Alfred A. Knopf, 1992 (originally published 1923).

Gladwell, Malcolm. *Outliers: The Story of Success*. New York: Little, Brown, 2008.

Gottlieb, Daniel. *Learning from the Heart: Lessons on Living, Loving, and Listening*. New York: Sterling, 2008.

Greeley, Andrew. *The Catholic Imagination*. Berkeley: University of California Press, 2000.

———. *Religion as Poetry*. New Brunswick, NJ: Transaction, 1995.

Gyatso, Tenzin, the Dalai Lama. *The Compassionate Life*. Boston: Wisdom, 2001.

Hanh, Thich Nhat. *Anger: Wisdom for Cooling the Flames*. New York: Riverhead Books, 2002.

———. *The Art of Power*. New York: HarperOne, 2007.

———. *Peace Is Every Step: The Path of Mindfulness in Everyday Life*. New York: Bantam Books, 1992.

Hirshberg, Caryle, and Marc Ian Barasch. *Remarkable Recovery: What Extraordinary Healings Tell Us About Getting Well and Staying Well*. New York: Riverhead Books, 1996.

Hoff, Benjamin. *The Tao of Pooh*. New York: Penguin, 1982.

Hofstede, Geert, and Gert Jan Hofstede. *Cultures and Organizations: Software of the Mind*. New York: McGraw Hill, 2005.

Ignatius of Loyola. *The Spiritual Exercises of St. Ignatius.* Translated by George E. Ganss, S. J. St. Louis: The Institute of Jesuit Sources, 1992.

Julian of Norwich. *Revelations of Divine Love.* Edited by Roger Huddleston, OSB. London: Burns, Oats, and Washbourne, 1927.

Jung, C. G. *The Collected Works of C. G. Jung.* Edited by Herbert Read, Michael Fordham, and Gerhard Adler. New York: Pantheon, 1953.

Keating, Thomas. *Invitation to Love: The Way of Christian Contemplation.* Rockport, MA: Element, 1992.

Kurtz, Ernest, and Katherine Ketcham. *The Spirituality of Imperfection: Storytelling and the Search for Meaning.* New York: Bantam Books, 2002.

Lerner, Michael. *Surplus Powerlessness: The Psychodynamics of Everyday Life and the Psychology of Individual and Social Transformation.* Amherst, NY: Humanity Books, 1991.

Lew, Alan. *Be Still and Get Going: A Jewish Meditation Practice for Real Life.* New York: Little, Brown, 2005.

Loring, Patricia. *Listening Spirituality,* vol. 1: *Personal Spiritual Practices Among Friends.* Washington, DC: Openings, 1997.

Malcolm X, with Alex Haley. *The Autobiography of Malcolm X.* New York: Ballantine Books, 1999.

May, Rollo. *Love & Will.* New York: W. W. Norton, 1969.

McLeod, Melvin, ed. *Mindful Politics: A Buddhist Guide to Making the World a Better Place.* Boston: Wisdom, 2006.

Merton, Thomas. *The New Man.* New York: Mentor-Omega Books, 1961.

———. *No Man Is an Island.* San Diego: Harvest, 1955.

Nolan, Albert. *Jesus Today: A Spirituality of Radical Freedom.* Maryknoll, NY: Orbis Books, 2006.

O'Connor, Elizabeth. *Our Many Selves: A Handbook for Self-Discovery.* New York: Harper & Row, 1971.

Ostrom, Warren. *In God We Die.* Pendle Hill Pamphlet 385. Walling-ford, PA: Pendle Hill, 2006.

Schachter-Shalomi, Zalman. *From Age-ing to Sage-ing: A Profound New Vision of Growing Older.* New York: Grand Central, 1997.

Seligman, Martin E. P. *Authentic Happiness: Using the New Positive Psychology to Realize Your Potential for Lasting Fulfillment.* New York: Free Press, 2002.

———. *Learned Optimism: How to Change Your Mind and Your Life.* New York: Pocket Books, 1990.

Sheeran, Michael J. *Beyond Majority Rule: Voteless Decisions in the Religious Society of Friends.* Philadelphia: Philadelphia Yearly Meeting, 1983.

Sifton, Elisabeth. *The Serenity Prayer: Faith and Politics in Times of Peace and War.* New York: W. W. Norton, 2003.

Simpkins, C. Alexander, and Annellen Simpkins. *Simple Taoism: A Guide to Living in Balance.* Boston: Tuttle, 1999.

Sogyal Rinpoche. *The Tibetan Book of Living and Dying.* San Francisco: HarperSanFrancisco, 1992.

Wallis, Jim. *God's Politics: Why the Right Gets It Wrong and the Left Doesn't Get It.* San Francisco: HarperSanFrancisco, 2005.

———. *The Great Awakening: Reviving Faith and Politics in a Post-Religious Right America.* New York: HarperOne, 2008.

Weil, Andrew. *Spontaneous Healing: How to Discover and Enhance Your Body's Natural Ability to Maintain and Heal Itself.* New York: Alfred A. Knopf, 1995.

ACKNOWLEDGMENTS

Writing this book has felt like a "leading," the Quaker term for something we feel called to do. The idea lingered in the back of my mind for nine years before the time seemed right. Once I began, serendipity often brought books or people into my life just when I needed their insights. This was particularly true of the nearly thirty people who agreed to be interviewed. I am grateful for their trust and great generosity in sharing their stories. Along with those who chose to use pseudonyms, I thank Jorge Arauz, Hilary Beard, Will Brock, Joan Countryman, Michael Doyle, Dan Gottlieb, Sharon Gunther, Erin Hirsh, Arlene Kelly, Hollister Knowlton, Marcelle Martin, Melvin Metelits, Ro'Bin White Morton, Malik Mubashshir, Eva Ray, Eileen Smith, Tracey Smith-Diggs, Hal Taussig, Peter Warrington, David Watt, and Celeste Zappala.

Thanks to my agent, Stephany Evans, who was the answer to a prayer. At Tarcher, I thank my editor, Sara Carder, for her enthusiasm for the project and her insightful improvements to the manuscript, as well as Katherine Obertance for her always speedy assistance. Sue Burrus, Mia Grogan, Michelle Humble, Amanda Kemp, and Tom Volkert also read parts of the manuscript and offered helpful comments. Chris Ravndal offered insights on the topic of discernment, and Sarah Whitman shared an experience of discernment. Thanks to all of you.

I am also grateful for the many, many friends who have supported and encouraged my writing over the years. Special thanks to the fabulous women of Wordspace: Hilary Beard, Meredith Broussard, Tamar Chansky, Miriam Peskowitz, Jude Ray, Andrea Ross, Eleanor Stanford, and our cruise director, Lori Tharps. You have all contributed to this book, one way or another. Although I do not claim to speak for Quakers in any way, I am deeply grateful to my faith community, Chestnut Hill Monthly Meeting, especially the committee that anchors my work: Christie Duncan-Tessmer, Nell Kahil, Signe Wilkinson, and Beth Zelasky. The community of Pendle Hill has continued to be a source of spiritual nurture. InFusion Coffee and Tea provided a different kind of sustenance, and a different kind of community. Claudia Vesterby and Alexandra Drobac Diagne got me out of the coffee shop every once in a while. Thanks to you all, as well.

I am grateful to my mother, Helen Flanagan, whose wise parenting I appreciate more and more in hindsight. I ask her forgiveness for writing about her when she is not here to object. I thank my spouse, Tom Volkert, for all his support and encouragement over the years and for being understanding whenever I needed extra time to write. Megan and Luke, thanks for being such great spiritual teachers. This book is dedicated to you.